CREATING
Ribbon Flowers

THE NICHOLAS KNIEL APPROACH TO DESIGN, STYLE, TECHNIQUE & INSPIRATION

Timothy Wright & Nicholas Kniel

Photography by Jeremy Harwell

D&C
David and Charles

TABLE OF CONTENTS

HISTORY OF RIBBON FLOWERS & EMBELLISHMENTS

Ribbon embellishments as we know them reached high art in the form of dress adornment in the seventeenth and eighteenth centuries. The latter was known as the Age of Enlightenment.

During this time, science, art and politics were of great interest to the worldly and well-dressed royal court of France, which was the epicenter of European culture and the birthplace of the Salon. The royal court of France alone established the latest European fashions. Many styles bordered on the obscenely decadent at a time when many citizens of France and Europe struggled with poverty. Both men's and women's clothing were adorned with dozens of yards of handmade ribbon trims and flowers, which could usually be moved from one elaborate gown or garment to the next. This happened frequently when a garment was worn out or needed a new look. Ruched and pleated ribbons trimmed the French court's extravagant gowns, stomachers and hats, which influenced the popularity of ribbon as an adornment.

The cockade, a pleated ribbon and a staple for military uniforms, became one of the most symbolic adornments during the French Revolution. Made from tri-striped blue, white and red ribbon, cockades were worn on the bicorne hats and elegant jackets of the French military. Its use spread to other European countries and found its way into everyday fashion.

Victorians created a whole language of meaning for flowers. Lovers and admirers brought tussie-mussies of real flowers to special ladies, who in turn would decode the hidden messages in the small bouquets. In addition, most women learned needlework and were often judged on their needle skills; excellent embroidery was the sign of a proper lady. At this time, the use of ribbons and flowers in fashion was less exuberant than in the previous century. The exception, however, was the evening dress. Gowns were still lavishly adorned with ribbon around fitted bodices and voluminous skirts of silk and satin.

During the postwar 1920s and 1930s, women became professional homemakers. Handbooks for the domestic arts taught women an array of skills for the home. One of the most popular subjects was needle arts. Ribbon became a readily available and affordable embellishment, making its popularity surge once more.

Before long, handbooks appeared that taught women how to make ribbon flowers and adornments.

Women could also order small handbooks out of magazines illustrating the latest ribbon accessories from Paris. Not only did these books give women ideas for their hats and clothing, but they also provided inspiration for their boudoirs and lingerie. Women could buy patterns for powder puffs, lingerie bags, eye masks, garters and other items and decorate them with ribbon work.

After a period of austerity due to World War II, ribbons again became popular for use on clothing. By the late 1940s and 1950s, ribbon flowers of all sizes were embroidered on evening gowns, jackets, shoes and handbags. Women's hats became small and compact, often adorned with little other than a simple band of fine ribbon, as in the pillbox hat.

As the first lady of the United States, Jacqueline Bouvier Kennedy brought back the cockade in the 1960s when she had one created to match her elegant day suits. She celebrated her French heritage in style with ribbon adornments.

Today's couture houses still utilize ribbon and other ribbon adornments for both evening and day wear. Ribbon is used in every conceivable manner on hats, gloves, shoes, suits, gowns and jewelry. Deconstructed fashions are not immune, as even those deliberately threadbare and worn pieces are sometimes laden with equally distressed ribbons.

The craft industry is well aware of ribbon's charm. It is widely used for a variety of crafts and artisan needlework. Ribbon has moved from the fabric store to the craft store and has found its way into fine gift and specialty stationery stores.

Ribbon adorns many things for humanity's life celebrations and holidays, such as gifts on one's birthday or at Christmas, Easter baskets and diplomas, or the simple twist of colored ribbon symbolizing the fight against AIDS or breast cancer.

Throughout history, ribbons have been used to adorn, celebrate and symbolize. The variety of ribbons available today is astonishing, both in range of fibers and of design. Their use in adornment, and for decorative or practical purposes, is limited only by one's imagination.

Getting Started

CHAPTER
ONE

SUPPLIES & TOOLS

Having the right tools and supplies for a project is essential for success. Here is a general list of some basic items that you'll need to have on hand for the projects in this book.

Ball-Head Pins

These are useful for holding pieces in place as you work.

Cotton Balls

Some ribbon flowers have parts that require a stuffing material. You can find large bleached cotton balls at most grocery stores and drugstores.

Crinoline and Buckram

Crinoline is used as a backing for many flowers as well as for layering sections of flowers. Buckram is heavier and can be used for the same purposes. These items can be found at most fabric or craft stores.

E-6000

This is an excellent glue used for attaching buttons and jewels to the centers of flowers (though vintage pieces should be sewn on, if possible). You can find E-6000 at most craft and sewing stores.

Fray Check

This clear glue is used to prevent fabric from fraying along the edges. Some of the flowers and leaves have raw seams that need a light application of this product, which can be found at fabric and craft stores. A little white glue thinned with water (50/50) works well, too.

Hot Glue Gun

The glue gun is a valuable tool, especially for applying pin backs and leaves and for attaching finished flowers to most surfaces.

Measuring Tools

A yardstick and a 12" (30cm) ruler will come in handy. An 18" (46cm) ruler is also useful to have around, and it is easier to handle than a yardstick.

Needles

The best needles for ribbon flowers are millinery needles in sizes 9 or 10. These needles are extremely sharp and flexible. If you can't acquire millinery needles, use whatever needles are comfortable in your fingers and easy to thread.

Needle-Nose Pliers or Tweezers

These are great for pulling the wire out of ribbon. The tweezers can also be used to help precisely fold and tuck ribbon when needed.

Scissors

Keep one pair of scissors for cutting unwired ribbons, one pair for cutting wired ribbons and a pair of embroidery shears to get in close to cut threads. Pinking shears are great for finishing the ends of ribbons, especially bows, and also for preventing ribbon edges from fraying.

Stamens

These millinery staples are used for the centers of several flowers. They are available in a wide range of colors. The three best colors to have on hand are yellow, black and green, as many real flowers have stamens in these colors. Stamens can be found at millinery supply shops or online.

Thread

Fine cotton and polyester threads come in a wide range of colors. Try to have a variety of colors in medium tones and hues. The basics to have on hand are white, ivory, black, yellow, orange, green, red, purple, pink, brown and blue.

Thread Conditioners

Conditioners prevent threads from twisting and becoming fuzzy, which causes knots. You can use a light application of beeswax or choose one of the various commercial thread-conditioning products available at fabric stores and craft centers.

Wire Cutters

These are used to cut floral stem wire and wire combs down to the correct size for your flowers.

On top: Hand-dyed silk satin, ombre taffeta, woven satin, woven velvet, striped taffeta, hand-dyed silk velvet.
On bottom: Dupioni, silk organza, grosgrain, taffeta, hand-dyed silk, jacquard, moiré taffeta, pattern taffeta.

Quality

One of the most important decisions to make when fashioning ribbon flowers concerns the quality of the ribbons used. You want to purchase the highest quality ribbon that you can afford for many reasons. Foremost is that the ribbon quality determines how nice or how shoddy your flower looks. Buy inexpensive ribbon, and you will have inexpensive-looking flowers. Use the best quality ribbons—acetate and rayon taffetas and bias-cut silk—and your flowers will look great.

Certain polyester ribbons don't look as nice or work as well for the techniques in this book, so check the fiber content before you buy.

Width and Quantity

The most common widths of ribbon we use are ⅝" (16mm), 1" (3cm), 1½" (4cm) and 2½" (6.5cm). When purchasing ribbon, a good rule of thumb is to buy 3 yards (2.7m) to make sure you have plenty. Most projects use 3 yards (2.7m) or less per project item, unless you're making soft goods or wrapping lots of gifts! For the ribbon flowers, 1½" (4cm) and 1" (3cm) are the two widths you will use the most, so buy extra yardage of these widths in various colors to have on hand.

Color

The number-one problem for most people is color choice. You should always buy what you love. If the color speaks to you, or it's your favorite color, then go for it. Also, think about matching or coordinating the colors you wear and the colors in your home. Purchase a variety of ribbons in different widths and colors to have on hand for any project that comes up. The basics include white, ivory, black, yellow, orange, green, red, purple, pink, brown and blue. Various patterns and stripes are also good to have available.

Dupioni Silk Ribbon

Dupioni is a bias-cut silk ribbon. Use dupioni to make Double Rosettes and Pleated Jewel Rosettes.

Grosgrain Ribbon

The best grosgrain is made from rayon or cotton. You can also use polyester grosgrain, but these are best for Bows and Cockades.

Hand-Dyed Silk

This ribbon is a bias-cut silk ribbon that is hand-dyed. It comes in a matte finish or a silk satin finish. Use it to make Carnations, Double Rosettes, Pansies, Pleated Jewel Rosettes, Peonies, Mums, Jeweled Mums and Silk Folded Roses.

Iridescent Wire-Edge Ribbon

This ribbon is woven with two different color threads, which gives it an iridescent look. Only use acetate iridescent taffetas to create ribbon flowers like Crinkled Roses, Leaves, Petal Flowers, Poppies and Pulled Roses.

Jacquard Ribbon

Fancy jacquard ribbons can be used to make stunning Bows and Ribbon Medallions.

Ombre Taffeta Wire-Edge Ribbon

Ombre ribbon has two or more gradient colors. Ombres are great for Cherry Blossoms, Leaves, Petal Flowers, Poinsettias, Pulled Roses, Orchids and Tea Roses.

Pattern Taffeta Ribbon

Taffeta can be patterned in plaids, checks and houndstooth. It can be used to make Bows, Cockades, Pulled Wire Roses and Ribbon Medallions.

Satin Woven Ribbon

Satin woven ribbon has a high, smooth sheen and is the most popular kind of ribbon. It makes excellent sashes and bows.

Silk Organza Ribbon

Bias-cut silk organza ribbon is great for making Silk Folded Roses and Double Rosettes.

Striped Ribbon

These ribbons come in all types: grosgrain, satin and taffeta. Striped ribbons are great for making Bows, Cockades and Ribbon Medallions.

Taffeta

Taffeta is a flat-woven ribbon, often with a sheen, and it is the most commonly used weave for wired ribbon. For flowers that require it, the wire can be removed from taffeta. With the exception of silk, acetate is the best fiber used for taffeta. This ribbon can be used for most multipetal flowers such as Tea Roses, Petal Flowers, Dogwoods and Poinsettias.

Velvet Hand-Dyed Silk Ribbon

This bias-cut silk velvet ribbon is hand-dyed. It is used to make Mums and Silk Folded Roses.

Velvet-Woven Ribbon

Use rayon velvet ribbon, if possible, for its supple quality. Nylon velvet also works to create beautiful ribbon flowers. This velvet ribbon can also be used to make Bows, Cockscombs, Hat Pin Roses and Mums.

TECHNIQUES

Many techniques are used to achieve different textures for specific ribbon flowers. By using these techniques, you will be able to create the desired texture for each ribbon flower.

Crimped Edges

Wired taffeta ribbons work best for the crimped edge. The technique is used for the Can-Can, Poppy and Cabbage Rose ribbon flowers.

1 Start with a length of wired ribbon.

2 Remove the wire on one edge of the selvedge. This will be the inside of the petal.

3 Stitch along the edge where you removed the wire with a basting stitch, then gather the ribbon loosely to the desired length. Don't knot off the thread yet.

4 Use your fingers to pleat the entire gathered edge of the ribbon, folding and pinching tightly. You may need to loosen it slightly as you go. Once the ribbon edge is crimped, pull any loose gathers and knot off the thread to hold.

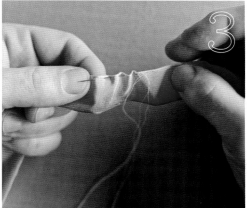

On left, from top to bottom: *Crinkled, cut loop, eyelash frayed, frayed, pleated and slashed.*

Crinkling

This technique is used on solid, iridescent and ombre acetate taffeta ribbons. It doesn't work on polyester taffeta ribbon. This wet technique creates the crinkled look for the Crinkled Rose variation of the Pulled Wire Rose.

1. Take the entire length of ribbon and plunge it into a bowl of cold water. Alternatively, you can hold it under a cold-running faucet to thoroughly wet it.

2. Lay the dripping ribbon out on a waterproof surface. Flatten the ribbon out in front of you, and begin scrunching it up tightly bit by bit from one end. Work your way down the length of the ribbon.

3. When you have crinkled the entire length, take the ribbon in your hands and crush it tightly into a ball, squeezing out any remaining water.

4. Gently tease open the ball of ribbon and stretch it out loosely. Allow the ribbon to air dry thoroughly.

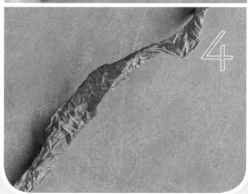

Cut Loop

The cut loop is used to create the Mum and Jeweled Mum ribbon flowers. You can use it on bias-cut ribbons of dupioni silk, hand-dyed silk, hand-dyed velvet and organza silk.

1 Fold the bias-cut silk ribbon in half.

2 Sew a gathering stitch along the ribbon about 12" (30cm) long.

3 Cut into the folded side of the ribbon with a sharp pair of scissors.

4 Repeat steps 2 and 3 until you reach the end of your ribbon.

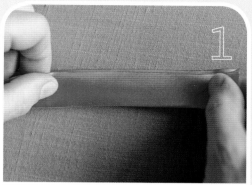

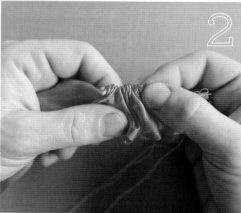

Eyelash Fraying

The eyelash fray is used to create the Coquette ribbon flower. It can be used with solid, iridescent and ombre acetate taffeta ribbons.

1. On the outside edge of your ribbon, trim away the very edge of the selvedge (this will also remove the wire on the selvedge edge). This will be the outer edge of your flower. Cut in a smooth, straight line, removing just enough to fray the ribbon.

2. Lay out the ribbon on a flat surface and gently pull out the threads down the length. Make sure the frayed edges are neat, with no stray threads.

3. Use a toothpick to carefully dab a line of Fray Check along the juncture of the frayed fibers and the ribbon. It's important not to load the toothpick with too much of the glue. It's okay if a little shows, but you don't want large blotches of Fray Check on your finished piece. Use a light touch. Allow all the pieces to dry.

Fraying

For ribbon flowers, fraying is done on bias-cut dupioni silk, hand-dyed silk and organza silk ribbons. It is used to create the Double Rosette, Carnation and Peony.

1. Choose the edge that you want to be the frayed edge.

2. Fray the edge by pulling the ribbon across the blade of a pair of scissors with one hand as you press the selvedge between your thumb and the blade in the other hand.

3. You can repeat this several times back and forth along the ribbon edge until you achieve the amount of fraying you want. Leave the other selvedge as is.

On right: The fray technique is used to create the rosettes for this stunning necklace.

Pleating

With this technique, you wet the ribbon and pleat it to create the Pleated Rose and Pleated Jeweled Rosette. Use solid, iridescent and ombre acetate taffetas, bias-cut hand-dyed silk and dupioni silk.

1 Start by thoroughly wetting the length of ribbon under cold water. Don't wring it out and, instead, transfer it still dripping to a waterproof work surface. You can keep a bowl of cold water on your work area or bring the ribbon from the sink on a saucer.

2 Start at one end of the ribbon and begin pleating it tightly with your fingers. It's best to leave the ribbon lying flat on your surface for this. Work your way along the ribbon, occasionally scrunching the accumulated pleats together on the work surface, until the ribbon is completely pleated. Don't worry about making the pleats perfectly even, as it looks best if the pleats are uneven. Now the ribbon will be a fraction of its original size.

3 Once the pleats are finished, lay the bundle of pleated ribbon on top of several layers of paper towels. Be careful not to undo the pleats. Tightly roll the pleated bundle up in the paper towels to blot any water and dye that may come out. Squeeze the bundle tightly to set the pleats even more. Unroll the paper towels and remove the ribbon. Thoroughly clean your work surface with a cleaning spray to avoid any dye residue.

4 Carefully open the pleated ribbon, stretching it out about 12" (30cm), and lay it out to dry. This can take anywhere from twenty to thirty minutes if the weather is not humid.

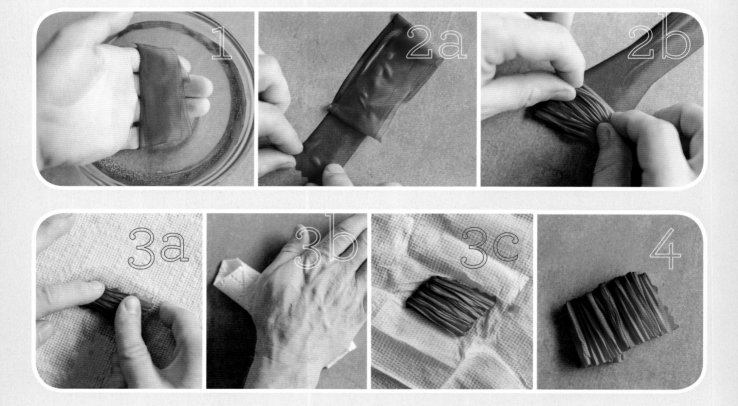

18

Slashing

We use this technique of cutting into the ribbon edge on bias-cut hand-dyed silk. It is used to create the Peony ribbon flower.

1 Use the fraying technique first on the edge of your ribbon.

2 Lay the ribbon out and, with a sharp pair of scissors, clip ½" (13mm) deep into the frayed edge about every ⅛" (3mm) along the ribbon.

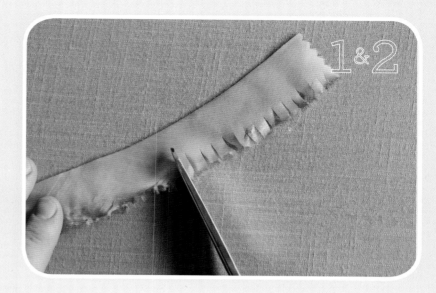

Above: *The pleating technique is used to create Pleated Jeweled Rosettes.*

FINISHING TOUCHES

As with many of the projects featured in this book, you can enhance or transform your ribbon flowers in a number of ways with the addition of the following embellishments and underlying structures.

Beads, Buttons and Crystals

You can apply beads or crystals to your flower creations to give them sparkle. New or vintage buttons can also enhance flower designs. Beads are generally sewn on but can also be glued. Crystals come in various shapes. They can be sewn on if they have holes or glued on if they have flat backs.

Feathers

Add small feathers to your ribbon flowers and adornments for whimsy. Create a dramatic look by adding larger feathers.

Floral Tape

This floral staple comes in many colors. Green, white, black and brown are best to have on hand. Floral tape is used to wrap the floral wire when putting stems on your ribbon flowers.

Floral Stem Wire

This wire is used to create stems for your ribbon flowers. Use 18- or 20-gauge stem wire when attaching stems to flowers for a bouquet. Use 20- or 22-gauge stem wire when creating smaller flower for boutonnieres and corsages.

Headbands, Hair Clips and Combs

Plastic or medal headbands are perfect for ribbon adornments. Hair clips are great for smaller flowers, and combs are ideal for creating larger sprays and groupings of flowers, especially for bridal use. Metal combs are preferable to plastic, due to their ability to hold more weight and withstand the rigors of creating headpieces from them. Metal combs can also be cut to size using wire cutters.

Millinery Leaves and Velvet Leaves

These can be used in place of ribbon leaves for a different look when added to ribbon flowers. They come in a wide variety of colors and can be found at millinery suppliers or online. New or vintage millinery leaves and sprays add an extra touch of realism and elegance. You can either sew these to your creations or use a hot glue gun if also adding a pin back.

Pin Backs

Pin backs allow you to wear your ribbon flowers or move them from one accessory to another, perhaps from a handbag to a hat. A length of 1½" (4cm) is generally a good size for pin backs.

Shoe Clips

Shoe clips allow you to completely transform the look of a pair of shoes without making the transformation permanent. Ribbon flowers can be sewn or glued to shoe clips, which are usually made of metal. They can be found at specialty stores or online.

On left: Shoe clips, crystal brooches, beads, buttons, feathers, pin backs, velvet leaves, hair clips, and a hair comb.

Adding a Pin Back to a Flower

materials

1½" (4cm) pin back

1 velvet leaf or a piece of felt

Hot glue gun

Glue sticks

Scissors

1 Trim the leaf or piece of felt to the correct size, if needed.

2 With the pin back facing you, open the pin.

3 Apply hot glue to the bar between the mechanisms at each end.

4 Press the leaf or felt to the glued bar to make it one piece.

5 Turn over the pin back and apply hot glue to the back, going over the bar and around the edges of the leaf.

6 Apply to the back of the flower.

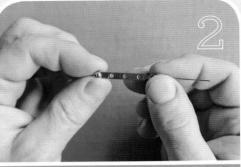

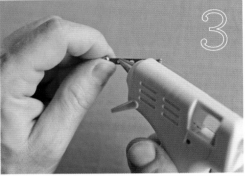

Adding Shoe Clips

materials

1 pair of shoe clips

2 velvet leaves or a piece of felt

Hot glue gun

Glue sticks

Scissors (or pinking shears)

1   Open the shoe clips.

2   Trim each leaf or piece of felt to the correct size. Cut a horizontal slit in the center of each leaf or felt piece.

3   Slide the clip through the slit. Apply glue on the back and attach.

4   Turn over the shoe clip and apply hot glue all over the back of the clip and the leaf or felt. Position the covered shoe clip and apply it to the back of the flower.

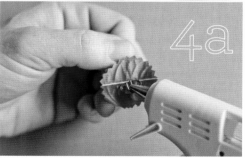

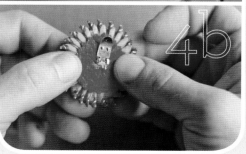

Adding Stems

materials

Floral wire

Floral tape

Wire cutters

Velvet leaves or felt

Hot glue gun

Glue sticks

Needle-nose pliers

1 Cut the floral wire to the desired stem length.

2 Using needle-nose pliers, bend one end of the floral wire into a hook.

3 Bend the hook at a 90° angle to the wire. This will help attach the wire stem to your flower.

4 Create a small hole in the center of your velvet leaf or felt piece.

5 Slide the wire through the hole until the hook lies flat against the leaf. Apply hot glue to the flat hook and press it to the leaf to hold it.

6 Attach the leaf and stem to the center back of your flower using hot glue.

7 Starting from the top, wrap your stem with the floral tape.

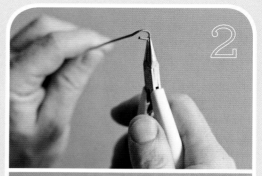

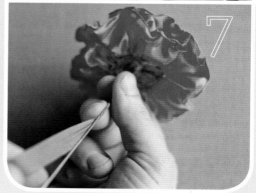

No need to panic! Here are a few tips that may help you fix a ribbon snafu. And remember, if you get frustrated with a project, take a break for at least fifteen minutes. It can do wonders!

Broken Thread

Stop where you are and knot off the thread, if you can, to hold your previous stitches. Start at that same point with a freshly threaded needle. If the thread is long enough and the needle's eye is big enough, rethread the needle with both threads and keep stitching.

Blood on Your Ribbon

Sometimes your finger gets in the way of your needle. Timing is the key to foiling blood stains, so act quickly because dried blood is much more difficult to remove than fresh blood. If the spot is too large or in the wrong place to be hidden, the enzymes in your saliva will help break up the stain. Rub some into the stain with your finger, then apply a bit of water with a cotton swab. Apart from that, a quick, judicious application of mild soap and water will help.

Frayed Selvedge

The selvedge on a ribbon can fray when certain threads at the raw (cut) end are pulled loose and accidentally drawn down the selvedge. Immediately isolate the fray, clip away any hanging threads and dab Fray Check on the spot to prevent further fraying.

Knot in Your Thread

Avoid knots by using thread lengths no longer than 18" (46cm) and by using a thread conditioner such as beeswax or Thread Heaven. If you do get a knot that you can't untangle, clip away the needle at the knot and double-thread your needle with the remaining thread (hopefully you will have enough to finish). No one likes to pull stitches and restitch a flower, but it can be done as a last resort.

Wire Breaks

If you are using wired ribbon and the wire breaks during gathering, simply push the remaining wire out of the selvedge where it has broken and continue gathering from that point. Clip away all but ¼" (6mm) of the wire and fold it over on itself to hold it. Using a double-threaded needle, start a knot on the selvedge, enclosing the wire to secure it. Start stitching back up the length of the ribbon where the wire broke and gather it down to the wire.

CHAPTER TWO

Flowers from A to Z

BASIC LEAF

This leaf design has been around for quite a while. It's often called the boat leaf, due to its boat-like shape when folded for stitching. It goes with almost any of the flowers, and you can use wired or unwired taffeta, silk, satin, velvet, even grosgrain and organdy. The leaf color can be any you choose, but a medium-to-dark green ribbon color works well with most flowers.

materials

6" (15cm) of ⅝"-wide (16mm-wide) ribbon for a small leaf

9" (23cm) of 1"-wide (3cm-wide) ribbon for a medium leaf

13½" (34cm) of 1½"-wide (4cm-wide) ribbon for a large leaf

Matching thread

Needle

Fray Check

If you're using wired taffeta or satin, remove one wire from the inside selvedge, where you will stitch. Leave the wire intact on the selvedge for the outer edge of the leaf. If you are using unwired ribbon, you will stitch the edge of the ribbon that will be in the center of your leaf.

1 Lay the length of ribbon out flat, with the wired edge at the bottom, closest to you. Fold the ribbon in half lengthwise with ride sides facing; the raw ends should meet.

2 Fold down both layers of ribbon at each end to create a 45° angle. You can pin the folds in place, if necessary, in order to hold them together while you stitch. If you're using velvet, don't worry about folding it—it's too thick. Just create a stitch line to follow.

3 Using a double-threaded needle, start a knot about ⅛" (3mm) up from the point of the fold on the right end of the ribbon. Make sure the knot is on the fold, not the wired selvedge at the point.

   Begin stitching up the fold, sewing through all four layers. When you're almost to the top of the incline, make a backstitch by making two stitches, one over the other. Then stitch along the top and down the other fold. This keeps the leaf point from gathering yet allows the rest of the leaf to be gathered. This is the only backstitch you'll do for this leaf.

4 After stitching, gather all the stitches and knot the threads securely. Clip away the needle and thread. Fold the tab of ribbon hanging on the pointed end over to the seam. Tack it to the seam to hold. Trim away the extra ribbon at the gathered end, taking care not to cut into the leaf or the stitches you've made. If you are using a thick ribbon such as velvet, trim away the excess of both folds once it's stitched and gathered, then apply a fraying preventive such as Fray Check to the raw edges. Open the leaf and flatten out the pointed end.

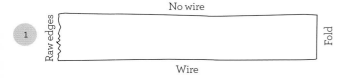

1 No wire / Fold / Raw edges / Wire

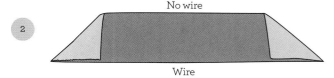

2 No wire / Wire

3 Back stitch / Start here

4a Gather

4b Fold tab over to seam and tack

4c Open

BOWS

When one thinks of ribbon, bows come to mind first. They are the most common items created from ribbon, and they adorn a multitude of things from gifts and clothing to hair and home goods. The simple bow sets ordinary objects apart as something special, celebratory or symbolic. This particular bow is stitched rather than tied so it can be used as an adornment on a variety of things. You can make either a classic two-loop bow or one with four loops. Any kind of ribbon will do.

materials

11½" (29cm) of ribbon for a two-loop bow

22½" (56cm) of ribbon for a four-loop bow

Matching thread

Needle

1 For the two-loop bow, cut 9" (23cm) of the ribbon for the loops; the remaining 2½" (6cm) is used for the center knot. For a double-loop bow, cut two 10" (25cm) lengths for each set of loops; the remaining ribbon will be used for the center.

2 Take the length of ribbon for the loops and overlap the ends by ½" (13mm), creating a circle. Find the center point and pin the ribbon together, creating two loops on either side of the pin. Using double threads, stitch through all the layers and remove the pin. Gather the ribbon, wrapping your needle and thread around once or twice to hold the gathers tight before knotting off securely. If creating a single bow (2 loops), continue to step 3. If creating a double bow (4 loops), repeat this process to create a second set of loops.

3 Take the 2½" (6cm) length of ribbon, create a fold down its length and stitch it to the center back of the loops. Wrap it around the front and over your gathers to the back again. Fold under the raw edge before stitching it down; if there is a lot of excess ribbon, trim away as necessary so the back will be flat when stitched down.

4 For the double bow, overlap one set of gathered loops slightly over the other set, and tack them together in the center before adding the center piece.

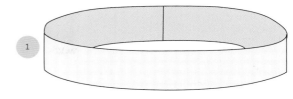

1

Make a tube

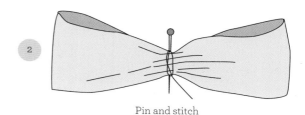

2

Pin and stitch

3a

Create a fold

3b

Stitch the center from the back

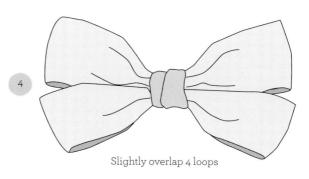

4

Slightly overlap 4 loops

CABBAGE ROSE

This flower was one of many ribbon adornments popular during the early part of the last century, gracing the delicate gowns and day dresses of the early 1920s. These roses tend to be slightly asymmetrical and are beautiful alone or in a grouping with or without the outer ruffles. They are outstanding as a pin when the ruffled edge is added as a contrast. This flower is best made with taffeta, but you can also use satin and velvet.

materials

1 yd. (.9m) of 1"-wide (3cm-wide) taffeta ribbon, wires removed

1 yd. (.9m) of 1"-wide (3cm-wide) wired taffeta

Buckram (crinoline works just as well)

Medium-size cotton balls

Needle

Matching thread

1 Using the pattern below, cut a 3" (8cm) circle of buckram. Make the circle into a cone by cutting from one edge to the center as shown. Overlap the two cut edges by about 1" (3cm) to make a shallow cone and, using double threads (1 yd. [.9m] folded to 18" [46cm]), stitch them together to secure. Knot the threads, but leave them attached. It's time to start tacking.

2 Take your ribbon and fold it over by 1" (3cm) on one end. Crease the fold using your fingernail, then open the ribbon. The resulting square at the end will help to correctly place the ribbon on the buckram cone when starting. Center the square over the point of the cone and tack twice on each of the four corners coming up from underneath and going back down from the top through the ribbon and buckram.

Pattern

2a   1" (3cm)   Fold

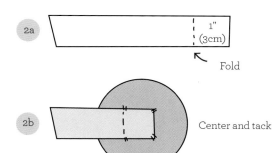

2b   Center and tack

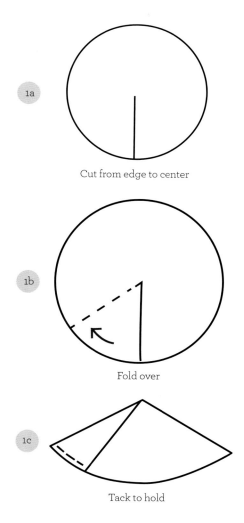

1a   Cut from edge to center

1b   Fold over

1c   Tack to hold

3 Once the four corners are secure, slide the ribbon counterclockwise a single turn to create a diagonal fold from one corner to the next, almost like a hospital corner. The key is not to turn the ribbon over to make the fold, but to keep the same side of the ribbon facing upward by sliding it across itself. Tack the two corners twice each to secure, and slide the ribbon another turn to make a second diagonal fold. Tack as before, and continue in this fashion.

The threads on the underside of your cone will create an open network much like the rafters in a barn. When your thread runs low, simply knot it off on one corner and start again with a knot on the next.

Though the rose will start off on the square, allow the folds to elongate and curve as you progress to accommodate the shape of the cone, thereby creating the layered cabbage-leaf look. Overlap corners as needed. Keep an eye on your overall progress and make decisions on folds accordingly. As you near the end, your ribbon may slightly overlap the edge on a few folds. When your cone is covered, cut away any excess ribbon to 2" (5cm) and fold it underneath. Tack to secure.

This rose, like many of the flowers in this book, will have slight variations from one person to another. Some people use less ribbon resulting in a softer, more open look, and others use more ribbon with lots of crisp folds. If you find you've run out of ribbon before the rose is finished, add more ribbon by sliding the end of a new piece under the last fold and tack. Continue with the new piece as before.

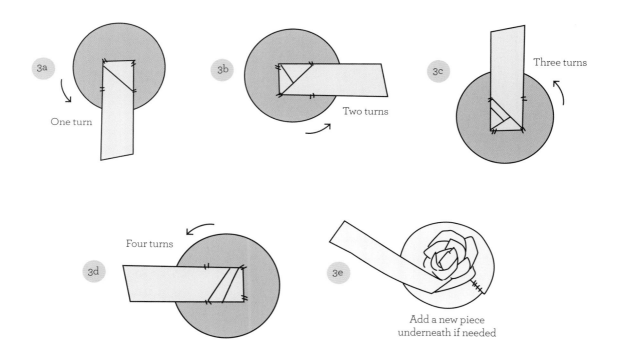

4. The ruffle adds a nice touch and serves to emphasize the rose. Take the yard (.9m) of remaining 1" (3cm) ribbon and remove one wire. Leave the wire intact in the selvedge that you want to be the outside edge. You will do your gathering on the inside selvedge that will overlap the edge of the rose itself. Using double threads, start a knot on the wired selvedge just in from the raw edge of the ribbon on one end. Stitch down the raw edge, then turn and stitch along the bottom, unwired selvedge to the other end and back up the opposite raw edge. The stitch pattern is below. Gather all the stitches, but don't knot off yet. You will need to stretch the gathered length back out to fit it properly around the cabbage rose after you have pleated it with your fingers.

5. Pleat the wired edge of the gathered ribbon at one end by pinching tiny folds into it with your fingers. Every seventh or eighth fold, crush them together to make them even more condensed. You want the pleats to actually look unevenly crinkled when you tease the ribbon back out to the size needed to encircle the rose. When you have pleated the entire wired selvedge, the piece will be a rather unsightly clump of pleats and gathers. Gently tease the pleats open while stretching out the gathers in order to make the ruffles the right length. Begin opening the pleats on the wired edge; the ribbon will curve with the gathered sides in the center. Lay the pleated ribbon around the rose to make sure you have extended the length enough that it wraps around the base and overlaps at the ends. If it's too short, keep going; if it's too long, draw up some of the gathers once more to shorten it.

6. When you have gotten the ruffles to the right size, knot off where the thread emerges from the gathers to hold them all in place. Take a medium-size cotton ball and place it in the cavity underneath the cabbage rose. This adds stability to the flower and makes it more crush-proof. Stitch the rose to a 6" × 6" (15cm × 15cm) square of crinoline, keeping the tacks at the outer edge. Once the rose is affixed to the crinoline, attach the ruffles around the outer edge, tacking only where the two meet. Place your stitches in the folds and crevices of the ribbon to hide them. Fold the raw edge under when overlapping the ruffles at the end. Knot off, and trim away the excess crinoline underneath.

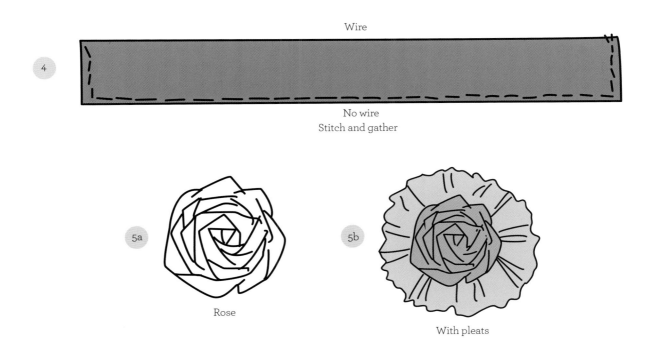

Wire

4

No wire
Stitch and gather

5a

Rose

5b

With pleats

We call this the Can-Can Crinkle Flower, because it looks like the underskirt of a Parisian cancan dancer. A unique-looking creation, this ribbon flower insists on being admired for both its beauty and its unusual design. For this flower, you can use wired taffeta in variegated or ombre. For the center berry, you can use taffeta, satin or velvet.

materials

2¼ yds. (2m) of 1½"-wide (4cm-wide) wired taffeta

Matching thread

Crinoline

Medium-size cotton balls

Needle

When making the Can-Can Crinkle Flower, it's best to make all the petals, then assemble the flower. There are eight petals (five outer and three inner) and one berry in the center.

1 Start by removing the wire from one selvedge of your ribbon. If you are going to flip the selvedges for color variations (when using ombre or variegated), cut your ribbon into nine lengths, each 9" (23cm) long, and then remove the wire from the chosen selvedges. If you're going to have the same color on all your selvedges, then remove the wire first and cut your ribbon into the nine 9" (23cm) lengths. You will have enough for eight petals and one berry.

2 Each of the eight petals is made identically in two steps. Take a double-threaded needle and knot off one raw edge about ¼" (6mm) down from the wired selvedge. Stitch along the ribbon at the same distance down from the selvedge to the other end. Do not knot off the thread or gather yet. Clip away your needle, leaving a 5" (13cm) tail of thread hanging from the ribbon.

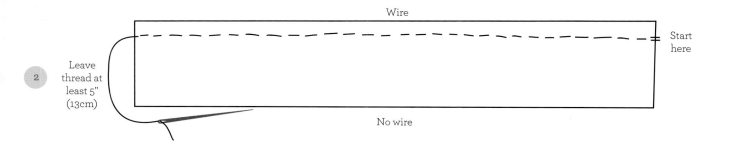

Wire

Start here

Leave thread at least 5" (13cm)

2

No wire

3 Make a second gathering stitch on the same piece of ribbon by starting on the wired selvedge and stitching down along the raw edges. Turn along the bottom and then back up the opposite raw edge.

Once you have completed the second set of stitches, gather them and knot off to hold. Clip away your needle, making sure to leave the other previously stitched thread dangling. Take your fingers and pleat the entire wired edge of the ribbon, folding and pinching tightly. The wired edge will close up when you do this.

4 Take the remaining hanging thread and pull it to further gather the petal. This helps make the crinkled edge even more pronounced and holds it in place while adding a pleasing "puffiness" to the petal. Tease the pleats back open while also loosening the threads you just gathered to allow the petal to spread open (about 1½" [4cm] wide). When you have loosened the pleats to your liking, take the hanging threads and rethread them on your needle, using it to knot off and secure the pleats. Clip away needle and thread. Make all eight petals in the same manner.

5 Take a 6" × 6" (15cm × 15cm) square of crinoline and tack the five outer petals in a ring at the center. Make sure to tack only in the center at the gathered edges and allow the sides to touch.

6 When the outer petals are attached, take the three inner petals and tack them in the center of the outer five. Space them evenly so, when you add the berry, they will pull up around it and meet side by side. As you apply each of the petals, line up its inner gathers with the inner gathers of the petal below it. Push your needle through both layers as you tack. Knot off tightly to secure.

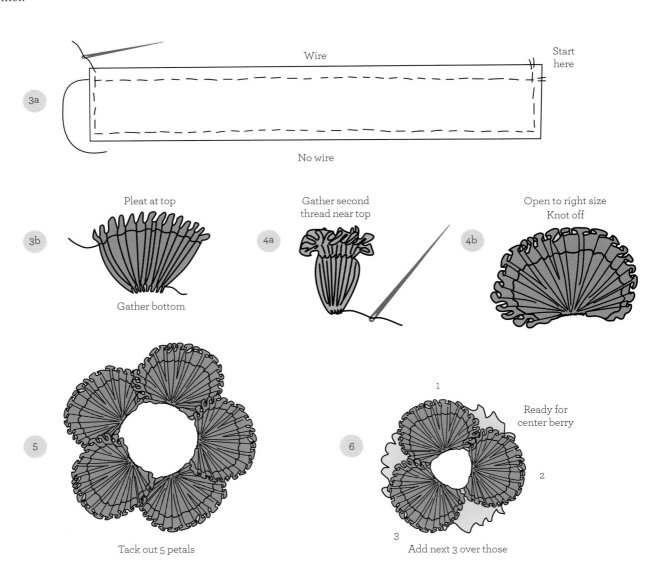

3a Wire · Start here · No wire

3b Pleat at top · Gather bottom

4a Gather second thread near top

4b Open to right size · Knot off

5 Tack out 5 petals

6 Ready for center berry · Add next 3 over those

7. To make the center berry, take the remaining 9" (23cm) length of ribbon and remove the remaining wire. Stitch the two raw ends together, using small, close stitches, to make a short tube. Leave about ¼" (6mm) seam allowance and don't gather. Knot off and turn the tube inside out while leaving the needle and thread attached. Start stitching around the circumference of the selvedge where your thread hangs, which will end up on top. The berry will be stuffed with cotton from the bottom. Stitch all the way around to where you started. Pull these stitches tightly and knot off on the inside, clipping away the needle and thread.

8. Start stitching along the other (bottom) selvedge in the same manner, and when you're ready to gather, begin stuffing the center with cotton a bit at a time as you do so. It takes about two medium cotton balls to stuff the berry firmly. Draw the stitches closed around it and knot off securely, leaving the needle and thread attached. Take the needle with the berry still on and run it through the middle of the center row of petals, pulling it down into the center. Come up from underneath the berry and tack it securely in place by angling into the bottom of its sides with the needle as you go back down. Tack all the way around its circumference in this manner, then knot off the threads.

9. A few tacks will be needed here and there to fine-tune the placement of all the petals around the berry. Come up from underneath with your needle and grab the inner edges of two of the petals at the same time. Push your needle down through the junction of the berry and the petals to pull them in tighter. It's best to eye the flower from different angles to see where you need to add a tack. If your gathers are peeking up in the center, pull them in with some stitches to hide them.

Once the Can-Can Crinkle Flower is stitched down securely, trim away the crinoline from the underside to finish.

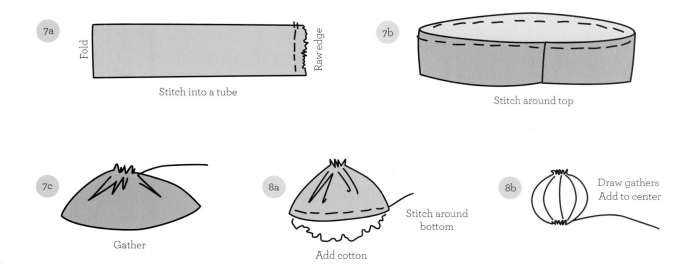

7a Fold Raw edge
Stitch into a tube

7b
Stitch around top

7c
Gather

8a
Stitch around bottom
Add cotton

8b
Draw gathers
Add to center

CARNATION

The Carnation is one of the simplest, yet loveliest, of flowers. The smaller ones are frequently scented with a deliciously spicy fragrance and come in an array of colors. Feel free to experiment with ribbon color on this easy-to-create flower, but use silk ribbon—it's the best for creating the delicate ruffles. The crisp white ones look remarkably real in the lapel of a tuxedo.

materials

1½ yds. (1.4m) of 1"-wide (3cm-wide) silk ribbon for a small Carnation

or

2 yds. (1.8m) of 1½"-wide (4cm-wide) silk ribbon for a large Carnation

Matching thread

Needle

1. If there is a color variation in your ribbon, decide which selvedge will be the top part of the flower (most visible). Take a pair of very sharp scissors and run one blade along the chosen selvedge of the ribbon. Don't be afraid to "ruin" the edge of your ribbon; you want it to be feathered well. Some small tears are unavoidable and add to the realism of the flower, but to avoid large rips, keep the swipe of the blade on the ribbon firm yet gentle. The bottom selvedge remains unfrayed.

2. Using double threads, start a knot on the bottom right end of the ribbon, ¼" (6mm) up from the selvedge. Follow the stitch pattern below and gather as you go along. When you're finished stitching, pull all the gathers tightly and knot off the thread, keeping the needle and thread attached.

3. Start rolling the gathers a bit at a time, tacking securely to hold them in place. This process forms the body of the Carnation. Try to keep the underside where you tack the rolled gathers as flat as possible. The silk will have a tendency to slip and slide, creating a concave shape that results in an uneven look to the final shape of the Carnation.

   Once the gathers are all rolled and tacked, knot off once more to hold all in place. Use your fingers to fluff open the Carnation.

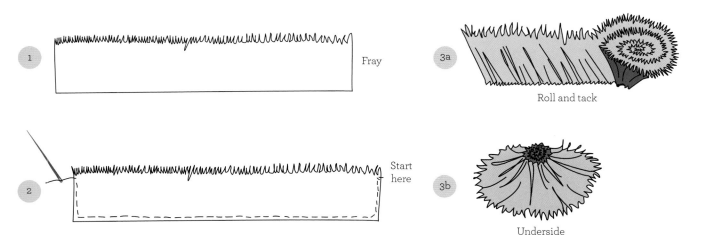

1   Fray

2   Start here

3a   Roll and tack

3b   Underside

CHERRY BLOSSOM

The technique for stitching the Cherry Blossom is also found in other ribbon flowers, such as the Pansy. You can create more or fewer petals depending on your needs. Almost any ribbon can be used to make this flower: wired taffeta, silk, satin, grosgrain and organdy. Use buttons, beads or stamens for the center. The lengths below are for five-petal flowers.

materials

5" (13cm) of ⅝"-wide (16mm-wide) ribbon for a small blossom

12½" (32cm) of 1"-wide (3cm-wide) ribbon for a medium blossom

18¾" (48cm) of 1½"- wide (4cm-wide) ribbon for a large blossom

Stamens or other items for the center

Matching thread

Needle

If using wired taffeta, remove the wire from the selvedge you want to be the inside of the flower, leaving the selvedge wire intact for the petal edges.

1 Take the ribbon and divide it into five equal sections. You can do this by making five folds and pressing each fold to make a crease. For 1"-wide (3cm-wide) ribbon, these sections will be 2½" (6cm) each. For the 1½"-wide (4cm-wide) ribbon, these sections will be 3¾" (10cm) each. You can also use straight pins to mark each section.

2 Take a double-threaded needle and start a knot on the wired selvedge of the ribbon, just in from the raw edge. Follow the stitch pattern, looping your thread over the wired selvedge as you stitch up and back again. Gather slightly as you go along; this makes it much easier to pull all the gathers once the stitching is completed.

3 Gather all the stitched sections and knot off to hold, leaving your needle and thread attached. Use it to tack the two ends of the flower together to make it circular. Tack only in the center where both your knots are, turning them to the back of the flower. Once you have finished the flower, you can add your center. If the opening in the middle of the flower is too large, reduce its size with extra stitches.

Gathering

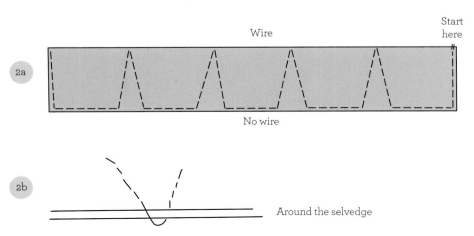

2a

Wire

Start here

No wire

2b

Around the selvedge

3b

Tack ends together
Close up center

COCKSCOMB

Cockscombs are decidedly old-fashioned, yet their unusual appearance makes them seem modern and exotic at the same time. There are few flowers more visually arresting than a large grouping of these amorphous blooms in a garden or a vase. Use velvet ribbon for the Cockscomb; it closely resembles the rich texture of the blooms. Classic wine-red is the prettiest color, but you can use yellow, aubergine, dark rose and even pale green. For a vintage look, try soft taupe to simulate old, faded blooms. The leaves can be made with velvet or taffeta.

materials

2 yds. (1.8m) of ⅝"-wide (16mm-wide) velvet for the flowers

½ yd. (46cm) of 1"-wide (3cm-wide) velvet

Matching thread

Fray Check

1 To make the body of the flower, cut the 2 yards (1.8m) of velvet into four 18" (46cm) lengths. Take the first length and fold the two selvedges together widthwise with wrong sides together. Using a double-threaded needle, stitch and knot the two sides together. Do this about ¼" (6mm) from the raw edge (cut edge).

Keep the ribbon folded as you go and run your needle through the selvedge from the right to the left. Move forward ⅓" (8mm) and push your needle from right to left again. The thread will cross over the selvedges. Keep moving forward along the length of the folded ribbon, casting your needle back over to the right side and pushing it through to the left.

Gather up your stitches every 4"–5" (10–13cm) as you go along, as it's difficult to pull stitches through velvet once you've stitched more than 10"–11" (25–28cm).

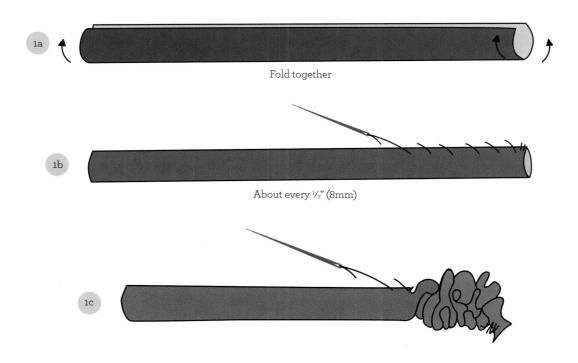

1a   Fold together

1b   About every ⅓" (8mm)

1c

2 After you have stitched to the end of the ribbon, pull the last gathers firmly to close them up and remove any slack. Knot off to hold, leaving your thread attached. Take the two ends of your gathered piece and knot these together as well, making a gathered loop. Knot off and put aside to make the next section. Complete all four in this manner.

2a

A loop

3 Once all the flower components are done, stitch them together one by one, making sure to keep the bottoms (raw ends) underneath. Twist and fold them around each other, tacking strategically. Don't worry about uniformity in tacking your looped pieces together. Cockscombs aren't symmetrical, which is part of their exotic charm.

3a

Several loops

4 For the Cockscomb leaves, cut the ½ yard (46cm) of leaf-colored velvet into two 9" (23cm) lengths. Fold these in half lengthwise. Use the same stitch pattern and method as for the Basic Leaf, but rather than fold the ribbon at the two angles on the ends, as instructed, use pins to mark them since the velvet ribbon will be too thick to fold.

Trim away the excess velvet after you've gathered and knotted off. Fray Check the raw edges and let them dry. Tack these to the underside of the Cockscomb so they protrude up and out from underneath.

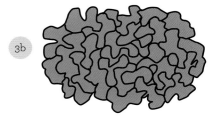

3b

All the loops

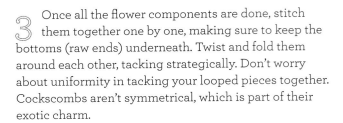

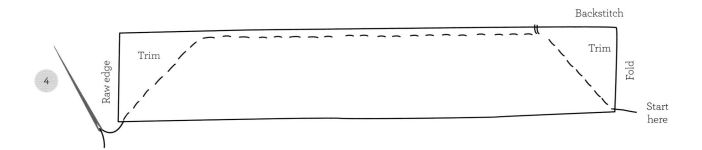

4

Raw edge

Trim

Backstitch

Trim

Fold

Start here

Create a Unique Corsage

This richly textured corsage can be worn on the wrist with a ribbon or on clothing for any occasion. Customize the colors as your attire or theme dictates.

materials

3 Cockscombs (or flower of your choice) in various shades of pink and fuschia

Pink velvet millinery leaves

1 yd. (.9m) of ⅝" (16mm) or 1" (3cm) satin ribbon in pink for the wrist and bow

Hot glue gun

Glue sticks

Pinback (optional)

1 Sew together the three cockscomb flowers to make a larger Cockscomb flower. Arrange them so they fit together as one.

2 Hot glue or sew the velvet millinery leaves to the back of the corsage, pushing some of the leaves through and around the Cockscombs.

3 For a pin corsage: Open the pinback and glue a leaf across the top of the bar. Glue it as one piece to the back of the corsage.

4 For a wrist corsage: Sew the finished corsage to the ribbon and use the extra to make a bow.

COQUETTE

Coquette is the perfect name for this beautiful, flirty ribbon rosette. The Coquette is perfect for a lapel, hat or handbag. The delicately frayed edges add a touch of exoticism to the petals. Taffeta ribbon is best for this flower.

materials

24" (61cm) of 1½"-wide (4cm-wide) taffeta for the outer rosette

15" (38cm) of 1"-wide (3cm-wide) taffeta for the inner rosette

6" (15cm) of 1½"-wide (4cm-wide) taffeta for the center bud

Crinoline

Cotton balls

Fray Check

Needle

Needle-nose pliers or chopsticks

1. Before sewing the various flower parts, you will need to prepare the ribbon. If using a wired ribbon, begin by removing all the wires from all three pieces. On each piece, trim away the very edge of the selvedge, which will be the outside edge of each rosette. Cut in a smooth, straight line, removing just enough to fray the ribbon. To fray each piece, lay it out flat and gently pull the threads out down the length. Use the measurements below:

- Outer petals (24" [61cm] length) fray ¼" (6mm)
- Inner petals (15" [38cm] length) fray ⅛" (3mm)
- Center bud (6" [15cm] length) fray ⅓" (8mm)

2. Make sure the frayed edges are neat with no stray threads. Use a toothpick to carefully dab a line of Fray Check along the juncture of the frayed fibers and the ribbon. It's important not to load the toothpick with too much of the glue. It's okay if a little shows, but you don't want large blotches of Fray Check on your finished piece. Just use a light touch. Allow all the pieces to dry.

3. Begin the Coquette by starting with the outer rosette. Take the 24" (61cm) length of ribbon and fold it into six 4" (10cm) sections. Press each fold with your fingernail to make a crease. You can also place a pin every 4" (10cm) for your seam line, if you prefer.

Use a double-threaded needle and start a knot at the juncture of the frayed selvedge and one of the raw edges. Stitch down the raw edge and turn along the bottom toward the first crease or pin. Angle up one side and back down the other. Make sure to catch the frayed edge in a thread loop over the top. Continue along the length of the ribbon in this manner, angling up and down the seam lines and gathering as you go along. The stitch pattern is shown in the illustration (bottom left).

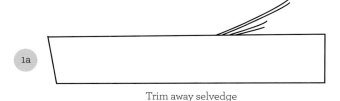

1a — Trim away selvedge

1b — Fray edge

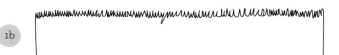

2 — Fray Check along this juncture

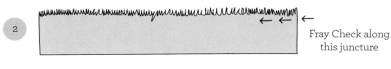

3 — Start here

Stitch and gather as you go along
Tack ends together to make a rosette

4 Pull all the gathers up and knot them off to hold, leaving the needle and thread attached. Tack the two ends together at the center, creating the rosette shape. Take a 5" × 5" (13cm × 13cm) square of crinoline with rounded corners and attach the rosette to it by tacking around the gathered center of the rosette. Knot off and clip away the needle and thread.

The inner rosette is made in exactly the same fashion, with the exception that you fold or mark five 3" (8cm) sections. Sew as you did for the outer rosette. Place this evenly in the center of the outer rosette and tack down.

5 For the center bud, take the 6" (15cm) length of ribbon and fold it in half lengthwise, right side to right side, if there is one. Using small stitches, start a knot on the unfrayed selvedge, just in from the raw edge. Stitch up along the raw edge to the frayed selvedge. Without gathering the threads, knot off securely, leaving the needle and thread attached for the next step.

6 Turn the piece inside out, pressing the seam flat with your fingernail to reduce any puckering. At the seam, start a row of gathering stitches about ⅛" (3mm) below the juncture of the frayed edge and the ribbon. Stitch around the circumference of the tube, keeping the same ⅛" (3mm) distance all the way around. When you reach where you began, gather the stitches tightly and knot off to hold. You now have a flat disc with fringe in the center. It's a good idea to knot once on the outside, then push your needle through and do a final knot inside (underneath) to hide it. Clip away the needle and thread.

7 Start a knot on the seam at the bottom selvedge. Stitch around the circumference next to the selvedge. Draw the gathers as before, but don't close them up completely. Take the cotton and stuff the cavity firmly bit by bit, drawing the gathers tighter as you go. Use a pair of needle-nose pliers or chopsticks to help you pack it tightly.

When it's full, draw the gathers as much as you can. This is the underside, so it's okay if a little cotton shows. Knot off securely, leaving the needle and thread attached. Use this to tack the finished bud in the center of the two rosettes. Clip away the excess crinoline to finish.

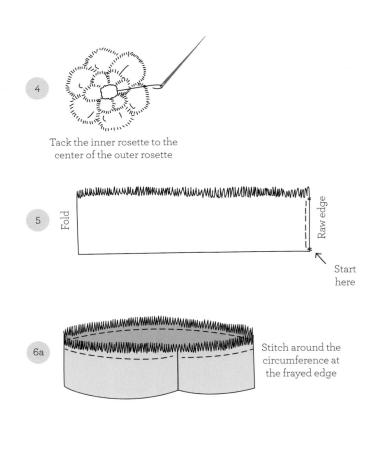

4 Tack the inner rosette to the center of the outer rosette

5 Fold / Raw edge / Start here

6a Stitch around the circumference at the frayed edge

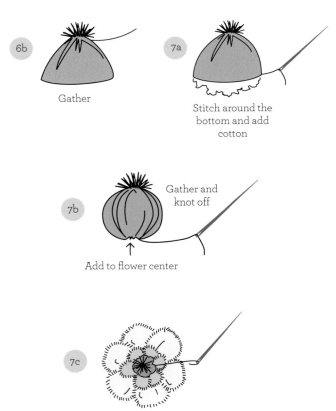

6b Gather

7a Stitch around the bottom and add cotton

7b Gather and knot off / Add to flower center

7c Tack the finished bud to the center of the two rosettes

On right: *Display your ribbon flowers on a custom tree. Take a foam tree form and cover it with fabric that compliments your décor year round. You can also change it seasonally if you choose.*

DOGWOOD

Many people think of Dogwoods as Southern trees, but in fact they are found around the world. Some of the Asian species are among the loveliest. Use wired taffeta for this ribbon version, which will look wonderful on everything from a bridal headpiece to a simple straw hat.

materials

14" (36cm) of 1½"-wide (4cm-wide) white wired taffeta

Chartreuse-colored stamens (or any light green)

Matching thread

Crinoline

Needle

Needle-nose pliers or tweezers

1. Cut the taffeta into four 3½" (9cm) lengths, leaving all the wires intact. Fold each of the four lengths of ribbon in half. On one corner of the folded end of the ribbon, take a pair of needle-nose pliers or tweezers and roll the corner over twice, about ¼" (6mm) both times. Use a single-threaded needle to put two knots in the center of the roll to hold it in place. Catch just the top layer of ribbon when making your knot. You don't want a stitch showing on the underside, which will be the front of your petal when finished. Roll and tack with knots at the opposite corner on the fold in the same way.

2. Turn the piece over to the front and pleat both sides in at the bottom by creating a fold and tacking it flat at an inward angle. This gives the petal a pleasing pucker that is very realistic.

   Turn the petal back to the reverse and place a knot about ¼" (6mm) down from the top of the fold in the ribbon. Again, catch only the top single layer of ribbon. Move down another ¼" (6mm) and take a stitch, pulling the knot and the stitch together to make a pucker. This pulls the top of the petal down into the familiar shape of the Dogwood petal. Make sure no stitches are showing on the front, and then knot off and clip away the thread. Complete all four petals in this manner.

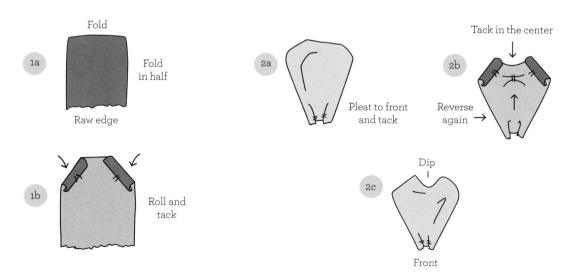

1a — Fold / Fold in half / Raw edge

1b — Roll and tack

2a — Pleat to front and tack

2b — Tack in the center / Reverse again →

2c — Dip / Front

3 Take a 4" × 4" (10cm × 10cm) square of crinoline and tack down two of the petals across from one another with the raw ends meeting in the middle. Tack them down securely in the center.

3

Tack down two

4 Take about thirty stamens and tie the threads of a double-threaded needle in the center of the bundle. Fold them in half and sandwich them between the two remaining petals. Allow the folded ends of the stamens to stick out a bit from the bottom. The heads of the stamens will point toward the outer edge of the petals. Take a double-threaded needle and stitch along the bottom at the raw edges, catching the two petals and all the stamens. Make sure to get the stamens securely stitched between the two petals so they don't slide around. Stitch back and forth several times, if needed. Knot off but leave the needle and thread uncut. You will use them to tack this piece to the first set of petals.

4a

Stamens

4b

Thread tied in the center

5 Open the two petals with the stamens and press the petals with your fingers to flatten them on either side. Take this piece and center it crosswise over the first set of petals. Tack them together tightly in the center, making sure the top set of petals doesn't sit up too high from the bottom set. Use strategic tacks to make them seem as much a single layer as possible.

Knot off securely and clip away the needle and thread. Arrange the stamens by pinching them in your fingers and pushing them down into the center of the Dogwood so they don't stick straight up. Carefully clip the finished Dogwood flower away from the crinoline.

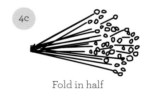

4c

Fold in half

4d

Tack between two petals

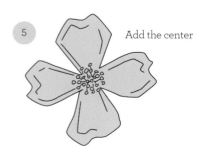

5

Add the center

Create a Classic Boutonniere

These ribbon Dogwoods are the perfect size for boutonnieres. They are amazingly realistic and will make a wonderful keepsake.

materials

1 Dogwood (or flower of your choice)

Velvet millinery leaves

Wire cutters

Floral wire

Floral tape

8" (20cm) of ⅜" (10mm) ribbon

Hot glue gun

Glue sticks

1 Cut a 6" (15cm) piece of floral wire and glue it to the back of the Dogwood.

2 Add velvet leaves behind the Dogwood flower. Using floral tape, wrap the leaf stem and Dogwood wire stems together by starting at the base of the flower and wrapping down to the ends of the wire stems.

3 Take one end of the ⅜" (10mm) ribbon and fold back about ¼" (6mm) and glue it to the bottom stem of the boutonniere. Wrap the stem with the ribbon, overlapping it slightly until you reach the leaves and Dogwood. Cut off any excess ribbon and glue the tail in place.

DOUBLE ROSETTE

The Double Rosette has a soft, vintage look due to its gathers and frayed edges. Use bias silk or organdy ribbon for this embellishment.

materials

½ yd. (46cm) of 1"-wide (3cm-wide) bias silk or organdy ribbon for the inner rosette

1 yd. (.9cm) of 1½"-wide (4cm-wide) bias silk or organdy ribbon for the outer rosette

Matching thread

Needle

Crinoline

Button or jewel

The Double Rosette consists of two rosettes tacked together: a smaller one tacked into the center of a larger one. Each has a French seam to hide the stitching. These rosettes look great when used singly as well.

1 Take the two lengths of ribbon and lightly fray one selvedge along the length of each one. If there is a color variation or a design in the ribbon, choose the edge that you want to be on the outer edge of the rosette. Create the frayed edge by pulling the ribbon across the blade of a pair of scissors with one hand as you press the selvedge between your thumb and the blade in the other hand. Do this several times back and forth along the ribbon selvedge, if needed, to get the amount of fraying you want. Leave the other selvedge plain.

2 Once you have frayed the outer edge of each piece, take the wider ribbon for the outer rosette and match the raw ends, wrong sides together. Make this piece into a loop by starting a knot on the plain edge and stitching the ends together toward the frayed edge. Knot off the thread to hold.

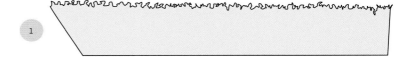

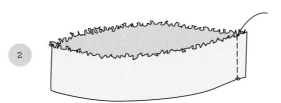

Start the knot at the plain edge and stitch the ends together toward the frayed edge

3 To create a French seam, turn the ribbon inside out and press it together with the seam at one end. Start a knot on the frayed edge just down from the seam you just stitched. Enclose the raw edge by stitching toward the inside selvedge. Knot off the thread securely to hold, leaving it on your needle and thread.

Open the ribbon and start a gathering stitch about ¼" (6mm) up from the inside selvedge. Stitch around the circumference of the ribbon, gathering as you go.

When you have finished stitching, draw up all the gathers to create the rosette shape and knot off to hold. Repeat steps 2 and 3 with the smaller length of ribbon to create the inner rosette.

4 Once both rosettes are completed, turn the seams to the bottom and position the inner rosette on top of the outer rosette in the center. Tack securely in the middle to hold them together. Tack the rosette to a 4" × 4" (10cm × 10cm) square of crinoline. Tack only in the center of the rosette where the gathers are.

5 Add a button or jewel for the center and trim away the excess crinoline from the back of the rosettes.

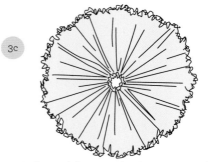

Gather and draw together into a rosette shape

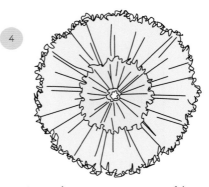

Center the inner rosette on top of the outer rosette and tack to secure

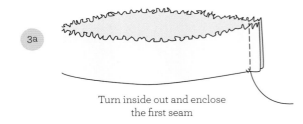

Turn inside out and enclose the first seam

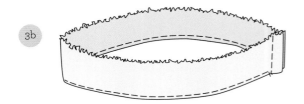

Stitch around the bottom circumference

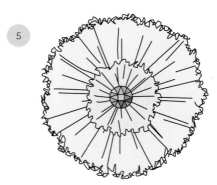

Add a button or jewel to the center of the flower

Create an Enchanting Bouquet

Full of delicate organdy rosettes, velvety leaves and millinery flowers, this bouquet is made all the more delightful with the addition of sparkling jewels.

materials

- 6 Double Rosettes (or flowers of your choice)

- 2 bunches of velvet millinery blossoms

- 2 sprays of velvet millinery leaves

- Wire cutters

- Floral wire

- Floral tape

- ½ yd. (46cm) of 1½" (4cm) double-faced satin ribbon

- 1½ yds. (1.4m) of 2" (5cm) or 2¾" (7cm) jacquard or satin ribbon

- Hot glue gun

- Glue sticks

1 Cut six 10" (25cm) pieces of floral wire. Glue one piece of floral wire to the back of the Double Rosette.

2 Wrap each stem of the Double Rosettes with floral tape from the base of the flower stem to the end of the wire stems.

3 Separate the velvet leaf sprays into smaller leaf sprays of three leaves. Separate the velvet millinery blossoms into twelve single blossoms.

4 Cut twenty-four 8" (20cm) pieces of floral wire. Using the floral tape, attach a small leaf spray and a velvet millinery blossom to each stem by wrapping them tightly down the length of the stem.

5 To assemble the bouquet, begin with the Double Rosette stems, then add the velvet blossoms and leaves. Wrap each of the stems to the others as you go with floral tape. After all your stems are taped together, arrange the bouquet by adjusting the wired stems as needed.

6 Take the ½ yard (46cm) of 1½" (4cm) satin ribbon and fold back about ½" (13mm) from one end. Glue the folded end to the bottom stems of the bouquet. Once the ribbon is attached, wrap it up the stems, overlapping the ribbon slightly until you reach the flowers and leaves. Cut off the excess ribbon and glue in place.

7 Make a bow using the additional ribbon and attach it to the bouquet.

FRENCH COCKADE

Various forms of the Cockade appeared on military hats and civilian lapels during the latter half of the eighteenth century in France, where the radical ideas of the revolution and its military culture permeated society. Today it remains today a military and secular adornment in Europe, worn to signify remembrances and holidays. It is also used for medals and as adornments worn with the Scottish national costume. You can use taffeta, grosgrain, satin or even velvet for the Cockade. A patterned or striped ribbon looks especially striking when made into a Cockade. Add a jewel or button to the center to finish the look.

materials

2 yds. (1.8m) of 1"-wide (3cm-wide) ribbon for a small Cockade of about 3" (8cm)

or

3 yds. (2.7m) of 1½"-wide (4cm-wide) ribbon for a medium Cockade of about 5" (13cm)

Matching thread

Needle

Crinoline

The Cockade is made up of points, each tacked together in the center to make a ring. Each point is made with two angled folds that are closed and tacked together. When working with the ribbon, you will always be folding up rather than under, so the wrong side of the ribbon is always enclosed.

It's easiest to make the Cockade from right to left, so you will start on the right side. If you are left-handed, simply reverse the direction.

1. Remove any wire from both selvedges of your ribbon. The best way to do this is to have someone hold one end of the ribbon between the selvedges, while you hold the other end taut and pull the wire out. If it breaks, push it out through the selvedge where it has broken off and continue. Otherwise you can gather the ribbon off the wire bit by bit in your lap, but you might need to iron it smooth afterward if it creases too much (use low heat or place it between clean cotton cloths).

2. Lay the ribbon out and fold ¼" (6mm) of the right raw edge over, pressing it flat with your nail. If your ribbon is one-sided, make sure the wrong side is facing up on the work surface and the right side is facing down.

3. For the first point, make a triangle by turning the previous fold down at an angle to the bottom selvedge and creasing it with your fingernail. Using double threads, start a knot on the selvedge where the two meet, and stitch them together to enclose the fold with the raw edge, whipping over the selvedge as you go. You are working toward the pointed end where you will knot off. This is the first of the two folds you will make for each point of the Cockade, but the only one you will have to stitch in this manner. Leave the thread and needle attached, as you will use it to tack all the subsequent folds and points together.

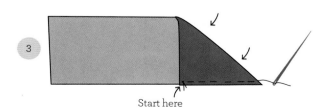

Start here

61

4 Once you have completed the first fold and enclosed the raw edge, you can make the second fold for your first point. Turn the left side of the ribbon down at an angle opposite the first one to mirror it. Crease with your fingernail. Allow a fraction of space between the selvedges when you make this fold so you don't get a pucker with the next step.

Close the two together and crease them. This fold mirrors the first fold you started with. Tack these together on the pointed end (where the thread is) with two good knots to hold.

For the next point, you need to start with another fold (remember, two folds equal one point).

5 Turn the length of ribbon to the left and crease, making the first of the next two folds. When you have made this fold, take it and fold it upward to lay on top of the first completed point. Now your ribbon will have the long length out to the left, as before. Turn the left length of the ribbon down at an angle once more, again mirroring the right side. Crease it and close the two folds together to make the second point. Tack them together with two knots, bringing the two finished points together in the process.

6 For the next and subsequent points, repeat the process. For each new point, start out with the long part of the ribbon pointing down and fold it to the left. Crease and turn this up over the previously made point. Turn the length of ribbon (now at the left) down again and crease. Close the two folds together and tack with knots to hold. Continue until the ribbon has only a few inches remaining.

All the tacks and knots are made in what will be the center of the Cockade. You will have twenty-nine to thirty points, depending on what type of ribbon you used. Velvet Cockades have a lot fewer points due to the thickness of the ribbon and also use less yardage.

7 When you have reached the end, take the tail of ribbon and insert it through the folds of the first point you made (opposite end) so it sticks through to the back side. This hides the stitching and makes the Cockade seamless. Join the two ends of the Cockade together in the center with knots to hold, making it into a circle. Adjust the tension of the joined ends by pulling the tail underneath to tighten it until it looks like all the others. Now turn the Cockade over, where you will finish it from the bottom.

Pin the tail inside the point it emerges from on either the right or left fold to hold it in place for the next step.

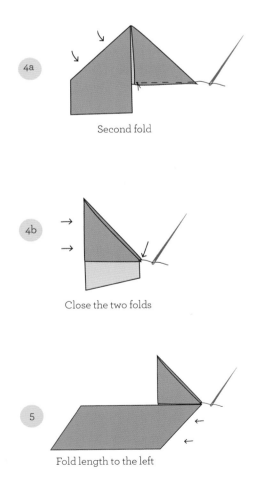

4a Second fold

4b Close the two folds

5 Fold length to the left

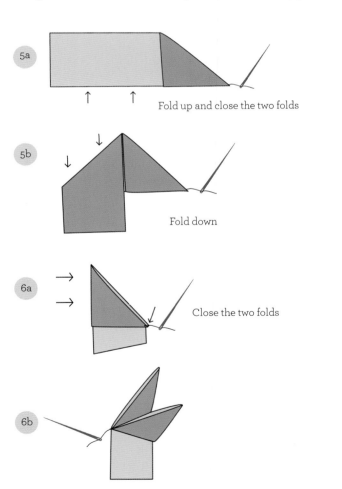

5a Fold up and close the two folds

5b Fold down

6a Close the two folds

6b

8 Take your needle and thread and tack the tail to one of the folds inside the point it emerges from. Make sure to catch the inside layer only, turning the Cockade over as you make each stitch to ensure none of these stitches will show through on the front. Once the tail is securely stitched to the inside of the first point, knot off and carefully trim away the excess tail of ribbon below the edge that is hidden.

9 Add a center, if desired. If the center hole is too large, take a double-threaded needle and start a knot in the center of the Cockade and stitch around the circumference, going through the folds. Stitch only in the center and gather the threads to reduce the size of the hole. Knot securely and clip away the thread and needle.

10 Tack a circle of crinoline or lightweight buckram to the underside; a circle of about 2" (5cm) is sufficient. Once the crinoline is attached, you have a base onto which you can sew a button or glue a jewel.

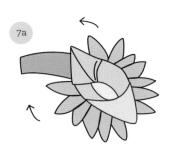

7a

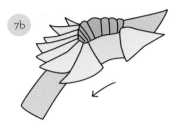

7b

7c

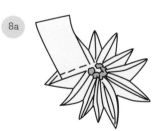

8a

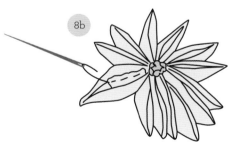

8b

If you want a flatter Cockade, lay it out and press on it several times with your hand, turning to the left as you do so. You can also tack it to the crinoline to hold this shape. Apply a warm iron using a cover cloth and press lightly.

GARDENIA

Heady, rich and alluring, these gorgeous crepe-like blooms have always enjoyed immense popularity. Billie Holiday wore them, and the Gardenia is associated with her image. Taffeta ribbon is ideally suited for the petals of this flower. Use pale ivory or crisp white for the most realistic ribbon gardenias.

materials

27½" (70cm) of wired 1½"-wide (4cm-wide) taffeta ribbon

Matching thread

Crinoline

Needle

Needle-nose pliers or tweezers

The Gardenia is put together with a set of inner petals made one way and a set of outer petals made a different way.

1 For the inner petals, take the ribbon and cut five 2½" (6cm) lengths, removing all the wires. For the outer petals, cut five 3" (8cm) lengths of ribbon, leaving the wires intact.

2 Start with the inner petals. Fold a piece of the ribbon lengthwise, right side to right side (if there is one). Take a single-threaded needle and tack several times in the same spot on one selvedge, about ½" (13mm) down from the fold. Knot off and clip away the thread and needle. Now place several tacks on the opposite selvedge directly across from the first in the same fashion.

3 Turn the piece inside out and flatten slightly. Two tucks will form on each corner of the fold. Start a knot at the bottom of the piece on the selvedge, just up from the raw edge. Stitch across the bottom and gather the threads to make the final shape of the petal. Knot off tightly to hold. Make the remaining four inner petals in the same way.

4 As you make the inner petals, create them, one after the other, on the same thread. They will be side-by-side at the bottom, and you will end up with a spiral of completed petals. Once finished, leave the needle and thread attached for the next step. If it is too short, knot off and get more thread.

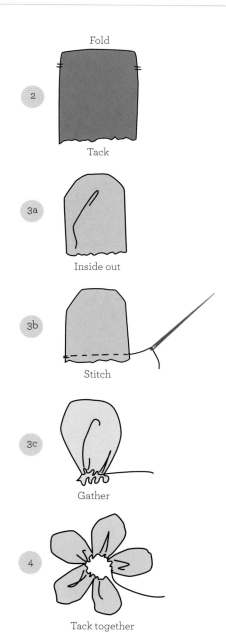

Fold

2

Tack

3a

Inside out

3b

Stitch

3c

Gather

4

Tack together

5 Fold the last petal together on itself, tacking at the bottom to hold. Roll the next petal around this first one, tacking at the bottom. Do the remaining three the same way, making sure to distribute them evenly around the previous ones. Tack each additional petal at the bottom of the others to catch all of them and make them one piece. Be careful not to allow the innermost petals to rise up too high in the center. Knot off the thread and lay the completed inner petals aside. Now it's time to make the outer petals.

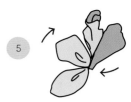

Roll and tack

6 For each outer petal, take the 3" (8cm) length of wired taffeta and fold it in half lengthwise. On one corner of the folded end of the ribbon, take a pair of needle-nosed pliers or tweezers and roll the corner over twice, about ¼" (6mm) both times. Use a single-threaded needle to put two knots in the center of the roll to hold it in place. Catch just the top layer of ribbon when making your knot. You don't want a stitch showing on the underside, which will be the front of your petal when finished. Roll and tack with knots at the opposite corner on the fold in the same way.

Fold

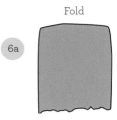

Roll the corners and tack

7 Turn the petal over and pleat both sides in at the bottom by creating a fold on the side and tacking it at an angle at the bottom. This gives the petal a pleasing pucker that is very realistic. Complete the other four in the same manner.

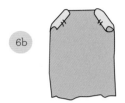

Turn over, pleat and tack

8 Take a 4" × 4" (10cm × 10cm) square of crinoline with the corners rounded and pin the five outer petals to it in a circle. Allow the sides of the petals to overlap slightly with the raw edges meeting in the middle. Use a double-threaded needle to tack each petal to the crinoline in the center where the raw edges are, securing the outer row of petals to make a rosette shape. Knot off and remove any pins, leaving your needle and thread attached.

Outer petals first

9 Place the set of inner petals in the center of the completed outer petals. Secure them at the base with plenty of tacks angled in toward the center of the flower to hide them. Pull the outer petals in with stitches, if need be. Knot off securely on the back, and carefully clip away the crinoline. Arrange the petals by turning the outer ones at a slight angle for a more realistic gardenia.

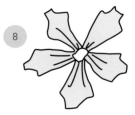

Add the center

Create Stylish Hairpins

These ribbon gardenias are realistic enough to fool the eye and to add glamour to any upswept hairstyle.

materials

- 3 Gardenias (or flower of your choice)
- 3 small hair clips or bobby pins
- Velvet leaves or a piece of felt
- Hot glue gun
- Glue sticks
- Scissors

1   Sew or hot glue velvet millinery leaves to the back of each gardenia flower, arranging them so they look good from the front.

2   Trim another leaf or felt to the correct size to fit each finished flower. Cut a horizontal slit in the center of the leaf or felt piece so a hair clip or bobby pin will fit through snugly.

3   Slide the clip or bobby pin through the slit. Apply glue on the back of the leaf and clip, then attach it to the back of the flower in the center.

HAT PIN ROSE

In past times, a lady would take a length of fine ribbon and tie it to a hat pin attached to her hat. She would then wrap the ribbon around the pin to create a stylized flower to wear for the day. Today these Hat Pin Roses are stitched to crinoline. Taffeta works best for this flower, but you can also use velvet, satin and grosgrain.

materials

30"–36" (76cm–91cm) of 1" (3cm) taffeta, or chosen ribbon

1 yd. (.9m) of 1½"-wide (4cm-wide) taffeta

Matching thread

Crinoline

Needle

1 Knot one end and tack down

1 Take the 1" (3cm) ribbon and remove the wire from both selvedges. Tie a loose knot in the ribbon, about 2" (5cm) from one of the raw ends. Take a 6" × 6" (15cm × 15cm) square of crinoline and round the corners. Using a double-threaded needle, tack the knot to the center of the crinoline from underneath.

2 Once the center knot is tacked down, wind the longer end of the ribbon around the knot in a half turn. Tack here and there in the crevices of the ribbon to secure it to the crinoline. Cover the short tail with the longer end of the ribbon as you wind and tack.

Allow the knot to show in the center when starting out. As you wind the ribbon around and tack it down, twist the underside up occasionally in sort of a flat spiral so the selvedges reverse (this looks great with a variegated or ombre).

Continue to tack in the crevices and folds so the stitches are hidden, making sure no crinoline is showing from underneath.

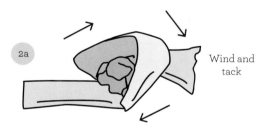

2a Wind and tack

2b More

3 When you reach the end of the ribbon, tuck it under some of the folds in the rose to hide it. Use strategically hidden tacks to hold it in place. Knot off and trim away the crinoline very carefully. Some of the stitches on the outer edge of the rose may show due to their placement on the crinoline. Trim as close as you can without cutting any of your stitches. If you have any crinoline that peeks from underneath or stitches that show on the edge, fold that edge under and tack from underneath to hold it.

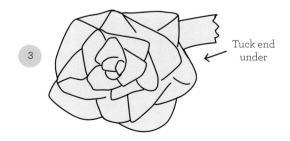

3 Tuck end under

4 Take the 1 yard (.9m) of 1½"-wide (4cm-wide) taffeta and remove one wire. Leave the wire intact in the selvedge that you want to be the outside edge. You will do your gathering on the inside edge, which will be under the rose.

Using a double-threaded needle, start a knot on the wired selvedge, just in from the raw edge on one end of the ribbon. Stitch down the raw seam and along the length of the ribbon following the stitch pattern below. Gather all the stitches, but don't knot off yet. You will need to stretch the length back out to fit the size of your Hat Pin Rose once you have pleated it in the next step.

5 Start pleating the wired edge of the ribbon at one end by pinching tiny folds into it with your fingers. Every seventh or eighth fold, crush them together to make them even more condensed. Don't be afraid to overdo the pleating—you want it to look unevenly crinkled when you tease the ribbon back out to the size you need. When you have pleated the entire wired selvedge, the piece will be a rather unsightly clump of pleats and gathers. Tease the pleats in the wired edge open while stretching out the stitched gathers. This will make the ruffles the right length to fit around the rose.

Begin the process on the wired edge so the ribbon will curve with the gathered sides in the center. Lay the ruffles under the Hat Pin Rose to make sure you have elongated it enough to extend evenly from underneath and overlap the two ends. If it's too short, keep going; if it's too long, draw up some of the gathers once more to shorten it.

6 When the ruffles are the right size, knot off the thread where it emerges from the gathers to hold them all in place. Take a 6" × 6" (15cm × 15cm) square of crinoline with the edges rounded and pin the ruffles in a ring in the center. Tack the ruffles securely, keeping the stitches on the unwired gathers. When you're finished, tack the Hat Pin Rose over the ruffles and hide the stitches in the folds. Knot off the thread securely and trim away the excess crinoline.

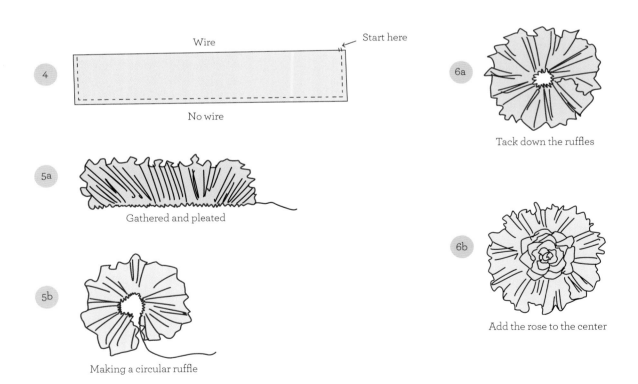

4   Wire   Start here

No wire

5a   Gathered and pleated

5b   Making a circular ruffle

6a   Tack down the ruffles

6b   Add the rose to the center

Create a Sophisticated Sash

Crystal appliqués create a sophisticated contrast with the Hat Pin Roses, making this sash perfect for cocktail or formal wear. You can also use a favorite brooch for a more personal touch.

materials

2 Hat Pin Roses (or flowers of your choice), omitting the other ruffle on each

1 crystal appliqué

5 yds. (4.6m) of 2"-wide (5cm-wide) ribbon

Matching thread

Needle

Crinoline or buckram

1. Arrange the Hat Pin Roses and the crystal appliqué onto a piece of crinoline or buckram.

2. Once arranged, tack the Hat Pin Roses and crystal appliqué to the backing. Make sure the stitches cannot be seen from the front.

3. Stitch the backed Hat Pin Roses and crystal appliqué to the ribbon sash.

HEIRLOOM ROSE

When we think of Heirloom Roses, we are reminded of our grandmother's carefully tended gardens. These hybrid roses originally came to the West by way of China and were crossed with native species. This yielded continuously blooming plants heavy with fragrance. These ribbon Heirloom Roses are made with delicate, bias-cut silk in soft colors.

materials

42" (107cm) of 1"-wide (3cm-wide) bias-cut silk for the rose center

2⅓ yds. (2.1m) of 1½"-wide (4cm-wide) bias-cut silk for the outer petals

Matching thread

Crinoline

Needle

1. To start the Heirloom Rose, you'll begin with the center. Take the 1"-wide (3cm-wide) ribbon and cut it into three 14" (36cm) sections. Each of these sections will be stitched separately and tacked together to make one center.

2. Using a double-threaded needle, start a knot on one selvedge, just in from the raw edge. Choose the selvedge you want to show as the outer edge of the petals. Start a running stitch down the raw edge, turn along the bottom selvedge to the opposite end, then turn up that raw edge to the top selvedge. Gather tightly and knot off, leaving the needle and thread attached.

3 Roll the gathered length of ribbon on itself and tack the bottom to hold it securely. Knot off and clip away your needle and thread. Lay this one aside and gather the other two lengths in the same manner. Once all three pieces are gathered, tack them together at the bottom to make one piece for the center of the rose.

4 For the outer petals, take the 1½"-wide (4cm-wide) silk ribbon and cut it into twelve 7" (18cm) lengths. Stitch these as you did the inner petals and gather them up, but leave out the rolling and tacking. Choose the selvedge you want to show as the outer part of the petals to start your knot on.

5 When you have completed the petals, begin tacking them around the rose center one by one. Tack the petals at the bottom securely, but don't pull them too tightly or your petals will look puckered and distorted. Start with three, allowing them to slightly overlap the center ruffles and each other at the sides. Cup the center within the first few petals. Space the next three between the overlaps of the first three, as shown below, tacking them also at the bottom. The rest of the petals are tacked on the same way, spaced accordingly.

As you add more petals, the base of the rose will expand, and you will find yourself tacking farther out from the original center. The petals will be more open, as opposed to being cupped at the center.

6 When you have attached all the petals, take a 5" × 5" (13cm × 13cm) square of crinoline with the corners rounded and tack the rose down. Keep the stitches underneath to hide them, and tighten them just enough to hold the rose in place without making it pucker.

When the rose is secured to the crinoline, adjust any errant petals with a few more strategic tacks and knot off the thread. Trim away the crinoline carefully.

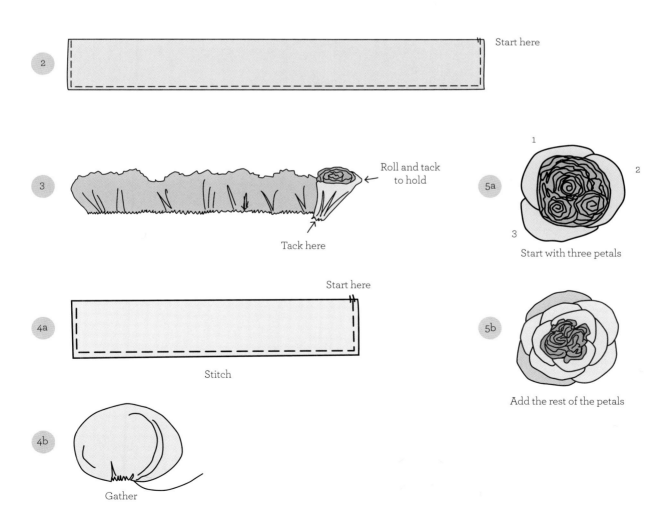

JEWELED MUM

The Jeweled Mum is a variation of the Mum. The addition of a jeweled center gives it a glamorous touch. Bias-cut silk ribbon works best for this flower.

materials

1½ yds. (1.4m) of 2½"-wide (6cm) bias-cut silk ribbon

Matching thread

Crinoline

Jewel or button for the center

Needle

The same steps used to make the Mum are also used to make this flower. Rather than rolling and tacking it together, however, the Jeweled Mum is tacked down to crinoline once the clipping and gathering is completed.

1. Fold the length of ribbon in half selvedge to selvedge, wrong sides together. Use pins, if necessary, to hold the halves together as you work.

2. Start a knot on the folded edge at one end using a double-threaded needle. Stitch down the raw edge and along the bottom for about 12" (30cm); don't gather.

3. Starting at the knotted end, clip into the ribbon from the folded edge down toward the stitches. Leave a ⅓" (8mm) margin where the stitches are, and space out the clips every ¼" (6mm) down the length of the stitched area. This creates the petals.

4. Loosely gather the stitches with the clipped petals, then stitch another 12" (30cm) along the bottom. Clip into this section as before. Gather again and continue these steps until you reach the end of the ribbon, then stitch up the raw edge of the end toward the fold. Creating the flower in repeated steps makes it easier to manage the ribbon.

5. Gather all of the stitches and knot off the thread securely. Take the gathered length of ribbon and pin it to the crinoline in a circle so it overlaps itself. Make sure the center is open enough to hold the button or jewel you will be adding.

6. Tack the Mum securely to the crinoline in the center. Add your jewel by tacking or gluing it down, and carefully trim away the excess crinoline on the back.

Stitch into a rosette

Add a jewel to the center

LADY'S SLIPPER ORCHID

Named for the shape of its shoe-like hollow lip, this beautiful, terrestrial Lady's Slipper Orchid is native to eastern woodlands. This ribbon version is best made with wired taffeta. The classic colors of the Lady's Slipper are pink and crisp white, but there is a yellow and white variety, too, along with striped and spotted hybrids.

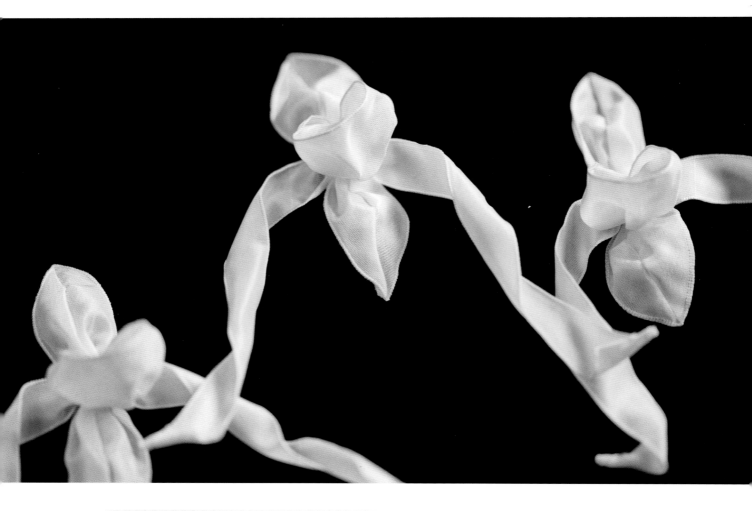

materials

10" (25cm) of ½"-wide (13mm-wide) or ⅝"-wide (16mm-wide) wired taffeta for the petals

9" (23cm) of 1"-wide (3cm-wide) wired taffeta for the sepals

4" (10cm) of 1½"-wide (4cm-wide) wired taffeta for the lip or "slipper"

Matching thread

Crinoline

Fray Check

Needle

The Lady's Slipper has two petals on each side and two sepals, one on the top and one on the bottom. The lip is added in the center.

1. For the petals, take the 10" (25cm) length of wired taffeta and cut it in half. The resulting two 5" (13cm) lengths will hang down either side of the lip, or slipper. Using a pair of needle-nosed pliers or tweezers, roll up one raw end at an angle on each piece, tacking discreetly several times to hold. At the opposite end, stitch across the raw edge and gather, knotting off the thread tightly. Lay aside to start the sepals.

2. For the sepals, take the 9" (23cm) length of ribbon, and cut it in half. Remove one wire, leaving the wire intact on the selvedge for the outer edge of the sepals. Fold both pieces in half with raw ends together. Using a double-threaded needle, begin stitching on the folded edge, just in from the wired selvedge. Rather than a straight line, create a slightly curved diagonal up toward the raw ends with your stitches. Use small stitches but don't gather. Follow the stitch pattern shown below.

When you have completed the stitches for the sepal, knot off the thread and carefully trim away the unwired edge of the ribbon, leaving a ¼" (6mm) seam allowance. Lightly Fray Check the cut edges. When the glue is dry, press the sepal open flat and start a knot at the bottom selvedge, just in from the end. Gather and knot off the thread. Repeat step 2 to create the second sepal.

3. To make the lip, take the 4" (10cm) length of 1½"-wide (4cm-wide) ribbon and remove the wire on the inside selvedge where you will stitch. The wire on the outer edge remains intact. Fold the piece in half with raw ends together. Start a knot on the wire at the raw edges, just in from the end. Stitch down the raw edges to the bottom selvedge, and then along the bottom toward the opposite fold. When you have reached the fold at the opposite side, stop and gather all the stitches. Knot off the thread and lay aside.

4. Take a 4" × 4" (10cm × 10cm) square of crinoline and round the corners. To assemble the Lady's Slipper Orchid, tack the sepals to the center of the crinoline vertically, with the raw ends meeting in the middle. Tack only in the center, where they meet. Take the petals and tack these down crossways, allowing their raw edges to meet in the center over the sepals. Finally, take the lip and tack it in the center as well, making sure the bulbous part is hanging down and the opening is visible. Knot off the thread securely.

5. Carefully trim away the excess crinoline. Take the long petals and curve them downward on either side of the lip, twisting them slightly, for a naturalistic effect.

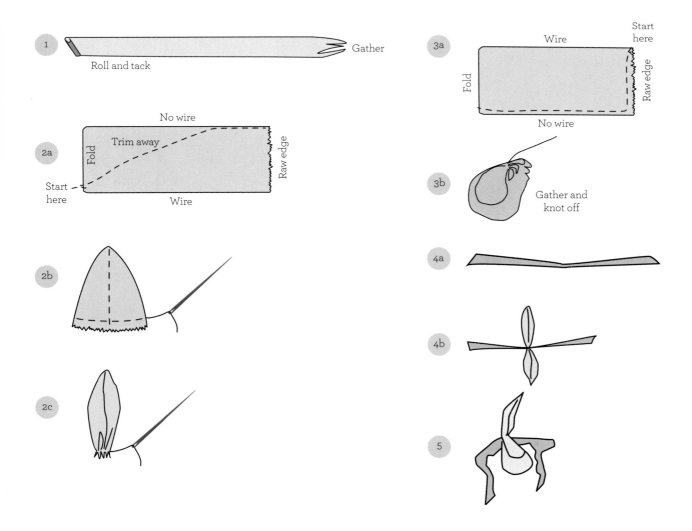

1 — Roll and tack — Gather

2a — Fold — No wire — Trim away — Start here — Wire — Raw edge

2b

2c

3a — Fold — Wire — Start here — Raw edge — No wire

3b — Gather and knot off

4a

4b

5

LOOP COCKADE

The Loop Cockade is a traditional type of cockade similar to those used for awarding achievements to the military, at equestrian competitions or at country fairs. It is similar to the Ruffle Cockade in that it consists of multiple loops tacked together. In the case of the Loop Cockade, the placement of the tacks is different and creates twenty-five points. Grosgrain works best for this cockade, but you can also use satin and taffeta ribbon.

materials

1³/₄ yds. (1.6m) of 1"-wide (3cm-wide) ribbon for a small cockade

or

2³/₄ yds. (2.5m) of 1½"-wide (4cm-wide) ribbon for a large cockade

Matching thread

Needle

Button or decorative center (optional)

For the Loop Cockade, you will add the twenty-fifth point using the tails of the ribbon after all the other points are made.

1. For both widths of ribbons place a pin 5" (13cm) from the raw end. This will leave a tail you can tuck in or trim away when you have completed your points.

2. The size of your cockade will determine where to place the second pin. If you are making a small cockade, measure 2" (5cm) from the first pin and place the second pin. For a large cockade, measure 3" (8cm) from the first pin and place the second pin.

3. Fold the longer end of the ribbon over the shorter end so the two pins meet. Take a double-threaded needle and tack the selvedges together twice to hold securely at that juncture. This is your first loop, or point. Remove the pins.

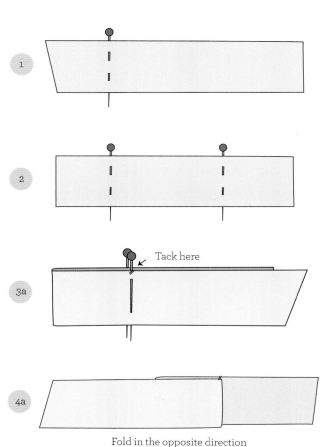

Tack here

Fold in the opposite direction

4 Create the next loop by folding the long end of the ribbon in the opposite direction and then folding it back toward the first two tacks, creating another fold identical to the first in size. Tack this at the same juncture as the first two tacks. Create twenty-two more folds (or points) in the same way, looping the ribbon back and forth on itself. Make sure the loops are as evenly sized to one another as possible. Use pins to hold groups of them together to keep them from sliding as you work.

5 When you have created all but the last of your loops, tack the last loop securely to the first one, creating a circle of loops. You will have two tails of ribbon left.

6 Take the tails and create the last loop by stitching one tail into the other. You will need to trim the ribbon to your loop size, making one longer than the other. Fold the longer tail over and stitch the shorter one inside it.

7 The side of the cockade with all of the tacks will be the underside of the cockade. Place the cockade on your work surface with the tacks underneath. The loops will flop open a bit, and you will see the beginnings of the cockade. Create the points by fanning the loops out into a circle, flattening it as you go. The cockade will take its final shape as you do this. Space out the loops so your points are even on the outside edge, then flatten out the inside edges of the loops as well. Use a warm iron with a covering cloth to press the Loop Cockade flatter, if desired.

8 Finish the cockade by turning it over to the underside and tacking all the loops to one another using double threads. Once finished, you can use the cockade as it is, or add a button or other decorative center.

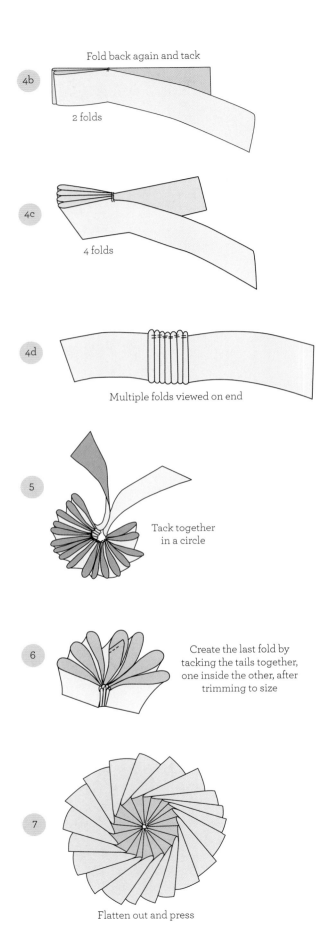

4b Fold back again and tack

2 folds

4c 4 folds

4d Multiple folds viewed on end

5 Tack together in a circle

6 Create the last fold by tacking the tails together, one inside the other, after trimming to size

7 Flatten out and press

Create a Striking Ornament

Cockades make anything they adorn special, and holiday trees are no exception. You can also create a gift bow, adding them to a special present as part of the wrapping; the lucky recipient then has an extra gift for the tree.

materials

1 cockade of your choice (image shows the French Cockade)

8" (20cm) of ⅛"-wide to ⅝"-wide (3mm-wide to 16mm-wide) ribbon

Hot glue gun

Glue sticks

Felt

1   Cut an 8" (20cm) piece of ribbon. Fold it in half to make a loop. Glue the cut ends together, then glue the loop to the back of your cockade.

3   Cut a small circle of felt to cover the loop ends on the back of your cockade. Use pinking shears for a decorative edge, if you like. Glue the felt over the loop ends.

MOTH ORCHID

The Phaleonopsis is commonly known as the Moth Orchid. Decorators love them with their tall, arching sprays of elegant blooms. They are usually white, but they also come in a variety of pinks and some yellow and spotted varieties. Use wired taffeta for these strikingly lifelike blooms.

materials

12" (30cm) of 1½"-wide (4cm-wide) wired taffeta for the petals

12" (30cm) of 1"-wide (3cm-wide) wired taffeta for the sepals

3" (8cm) of 1"-wide (3cm-wide) wired taffeta for the center lip

Matching thread

Crinoline

Fray Check

1 Take the 12" (30cm) length of 1"-wide (3cm-wide) ribbon and cut three 4" (10cm) lengths for the sepals. Remove one wire from each, keeping in mind that the wired edge is the outside edge of the sepals. Fold each piece in half. Starting just in from the wired edge on the fold of each, stitch at a curved angle up toward the raw ends, as shown in the stitch pattern on the following page. Do not gather, but knot the thread securely. Stitch all three like this.

2 Once the stitching is completed, cut away the excess part of the ribbon on the unwired edge, leaving a ¼" (6mm) seam allowance. Start a knot on one of the wired edges at the bottom, just up from the raw edges of each sepal, and stitch along the bottom to the other side. Gather tightly and knot off securely. Do the same for the other two, and lay all three aside.

For the petals, take the 12" (30cm) length of 1½" (4cm) taffeta and cut it in half to make two 6" (15cm) lengths. Remove the wire from the edge on the inside selvedge where you will stitch. For each petal, use the stitch pattern below, starting a knot on one wired edge. Stitch down and along the bottom, then up the other side. Gather tightly and knot off the threads.

For the center lip, take the 3" (8cm) length of 1"-wide (3cm-wide) ribbon and remove one wire, leaving the outer selvedge wire intact. Stitch the same as for the petals above. Gather tightly and knot off.

Anytime you have folded petals with raw trimmed edges, it's good to apply Fray Check to prevent fraying. Pour out a dime-sized pool of Fray Check, and use a toothpick to lightly coat the raw edges. Lay all aside to dry. Once the Fray Check is dry, open each sepal and petal, pressing the center seams flat with a fingernail.

The Moth Orchid is made starting with the sepal in an upside-down Y shape. Take a 4" × 4" (10cm × 10cm) square of crinoline and tack the sepals down securely with the raw edges meeting in the center. Tack only in the center parts for the assembly of the orchid. Next, take the petals and tack these two down over the sepals with their raw edges also meeting in the center. The lip is a small piece, but it should nicely cover the exposed raw edges of the two petals. Tack this piece securely down in the center.

Once you have finished tacking all the pieces down, knot off and carefully trim away the excess crinoline. You can fine-tune the arrangement of the orchid petals and crinkle the lip slightly by pinching in the two sides for a more realistic look.

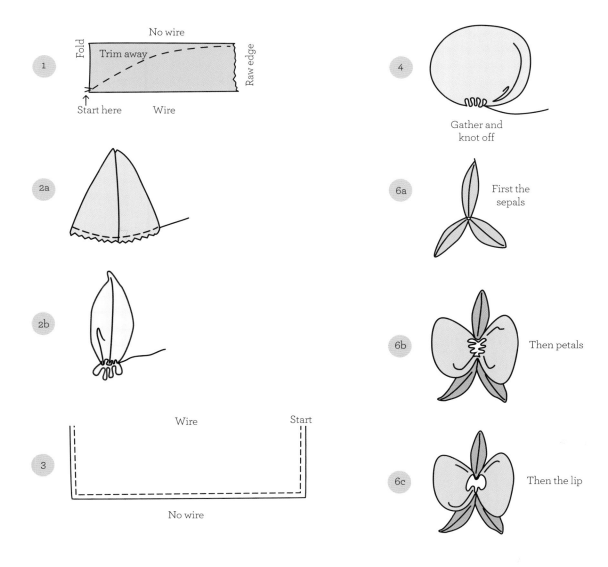

MUM

Mums are lush with petals. Like its real namesake, the ribbon Mum also has a multitude of petals that give it a very realistic look. The petals are made by snipping into the folded ribbon. Bias-cut silk or silk velvet ribbon works best for these flowers.

materials

2 yds. (1.8m) of 2½"-wide (6cm-wide) bias-cut silk ribbon

or

1½ yds. (1.4m) of 2½"-wide (6cm-wide) bias-cut silk velvet ribbon

Matching thread

Needle

1 Fold the length of ribbon in half, selvedge to selvedge, with wrong sides together. Use pins, if necessary, to hold the halves together as you work.

2 Start a knot on the folded edge at one end using a double-threaded needle. Stitch down the raw edge and along the bottom for about 12" (30cm); don't gather.

3 Starting at the knotted end, clip into the ribbon from the folded edge down toward the stitches. Leave a ⅓" (8mm) margin where the stitches are, and space out the clips every ¼" (6mm) down the length of the stitched area. This creates the petals.

4 Loosely gather the stitches with the clipped petals, then stitch another 12" (30cm) along the bottom. Clip into this section as before. Gather the stitches again and continue these steps until you reach the end of the ribbon, then stitch up the raw edge of the end toward the fold. Creating the flower in repeated steps makes it easier to manage the ribbon.

5 Gather all of the stitches and knot the thread securely. Take the gathered ribbon and roll it on itself, tacking it every so often underneath to hold it. Once you have completely rolled up and tacked all of the ribbon together, it will open up into a pom-pom shape like a Chrysanthemum.

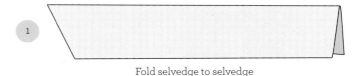

1

Fold selvedge to selvedge

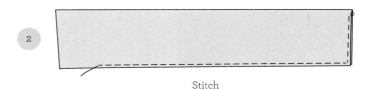

2

Stitch

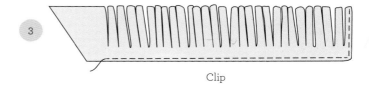

3

Clip

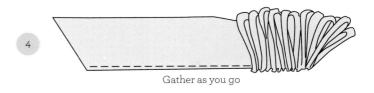

4

Gather as you go

5

Roll and tack underneath

85

PANSY

These realistic ribbon flowers look great in clusters. Pansies are classically purple and yellow, but they can also be made in russet, yellow, white, bright orange or even pale salmon. Delicate silk ribbon is best for these flowers, but taffeta and satin will do as well. Try making the two sets of petals in contrasting colors such as dark violet and crisp white. Such combinations add to the flowers' realistic look.

materials

- 10" (25cm) of 1"-wide (3cm-wide) unwired silk ribbon for the front set of petals

- 6" (15cm) of 1"-wide (3cm-wide) unwired silk ribbon for the back petals

- Stamens (bright yellow works best)

- Crinoline

- Matching thread

- Needle-nose pliers or tweezers

- Needle

1 Start with the back petals. Take the 6" (15cm) piece of ribbon and fold it in half to make a crease in the center, creating two 3" (8cm) sections. Using double threads, make a knot on the top right selvedge ¼" (6mm) from the raw edge. Using a gathering stitch, follow the pattern shown opposite to make two petals. Remember to angle your stitches up one side of the crease and down the other, looping over the selvedge at the top.

2 Do a final gathering and pull the petals tight, knotting off to hold them. Keeping the needle and thread attached, take the petals and tack them down to a small 2" (5cm) square of crinoline. Tack only in the center where the gathers are. Knot off on the reverse and clip away the needle and thread.

3 Take the 10" (25cm) piece of ribbon and fold and crease it to make three sections along the length. The first section should be 3" (8cm), followed by a 4" (10cm) section and then another 3" (8cm) section, as shown. Using double threads, make another knot on the top right selvedge ¼" (6mm) from the raw edge, as you did for the back petals. Follow the stitch pattern below for these three petals. Don't forget to gather as you go along.

4 Once the three petals are stitched and gathered tightly, knot off and tack the two ends of the gathered petals together to make a cloverlike shape. The center will have an opening to insert the stamens into.

5 Take five or six stamens and fold them in half, inserting the folded ends into the center hole of the petals. Allow about ⅓" to ½" (8mm to 13mm) of the stamen heads and stems to protrude from the front. Tack the center securely closed around the stamens from behind to hold them in place. Knot off again, and tack down the excess stamens protruding from the back by folding them down. You can also take a pair of needle-nose pliers or tweezers and roll them up, holding them in place and tacking them down securely.

6 Place the three petals with the stamens over the first set of petals already tacked to the crinoline. Make sure to have the wide petal (the 4" [10cm] section) pointing downward. About half of the rear petals should show from behind. Tack securely and knot off on the reverse. Carefully trim away the crinoline to finish.

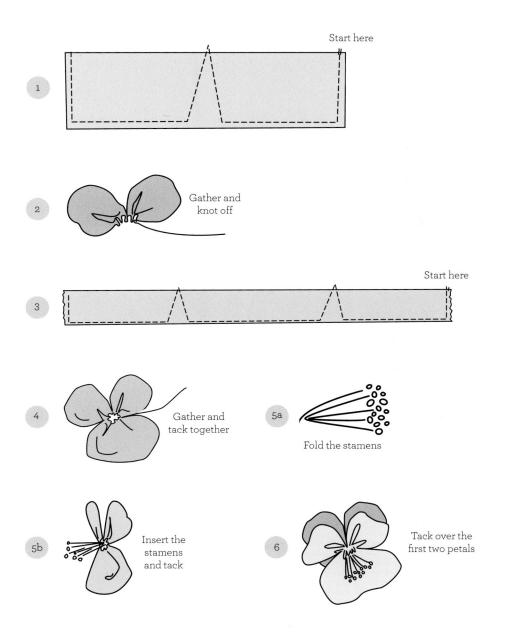

Start here

1

2 Gather and knot off

Start here

3

4 Gather and tack together

5a Fold the stamens

5b Insert the stamens and tack

6 Tack over the first two petals

PEONY

The Greeks named Peonies after Paeon, the physician of the gods, due to their purported healing properties. The lush blooms on these plants are rich with fragrance and come in various soft pinks, white and crimson. Bias-cut silk is perfect for this ribbon flower.

materials

2²/₃ yds. (2.4m) of 1½"-wide (4cm-wide) bias-cut silk ribbon

2 yds. (1.8m) of 2"-wide (5cm-wide) bias-cut silk ribbon

Crinoline

Matching thread

Needle

cutting

This flower is made with four rows of petals. Cut the ribbon into the following lengths for each row:

row one, 72" (183cm) of the 1½"-wide (4cm-wide) ribbon

row two, 24" (61cm) of the 1½"-wide (4cm-wide) ribbon

row three, 24" (61cm) of the 2"-wide (5cm-wide) ribbon

row four, 40" (102cm) of the 2"-wide (5cm-wide) ribbon

Rows one and two require the ribbon to be frayed along one selvedge for texture. Create the frayed edge by pulling the ribbon across the blade of a pair of scissors with one hand as you press the selvedge between your thumb and the blade in the other hand. Do this several times back and forth along the ribbon selvedge to get the amount of fraying you want. Leave the other selvedge for each piece plain.

1. Take the 72" (183cm) length of frayed ribbon and start a knot with double threads on the frayed selvedge at one end, just in from the raw edge. Stitch down the raw edge and then the bottom using a gathering stitch. Pull the gathers as you go along, following the stitch pattern in the illustration below.

   When you have finished stitching to the opposite feathered edge, pull all the gathers and securely knot the thread to hold. Leave the needle and thread attached.

2. Roll the newly gathered length on itself, starting at the end with the needle, and tack securely at the bottom as you go along. Make sure to keep the gathered edge evenly rolled (flat on the bottom, rather than concave or convex). Don't hesitate to hold the ribbon tightly in your hands as you go; crushing it will only add to the texture.

3. After you have rolled and tacked together the entire length, the flower resembles the Carnation. Knot off securely to hold. Take a 4" × 4" (10cm × 10cm) piece of crinoline and tack the gathered ribbon down in the center. Tack around the edges of the bottom gathers and place a few tacks in the center from underneath.

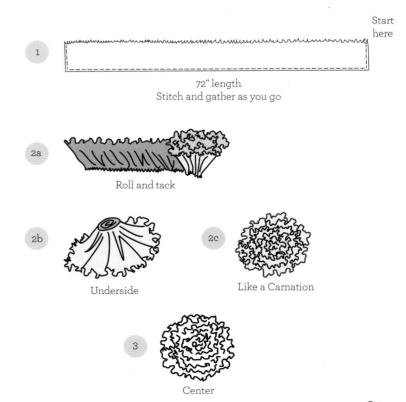

1   72" length
Stitch and gather as you go
Start here

2a   Roll and tack

2b   Underside

2c   Like a Carnation

3   Center

4 Row 2 consists of the 24" (61cm) length of frayed ribbon. Lay the ribbon out and clip into the frayed edge every ⅛" (3mm) about ½" (13mm) deep with a pair of scissors. Once you've clipped along the entire frayed selvedge, stitch this section as you did the first one. Gather as you go along.

5 When the stitches are completed, pull the gathers, but not all the way this time. Instead, wrap the newly gathered length around the base of the center piece so the ends meet. Finish pulling the gathers so they encircle it snugly. When it's the right size, knot off the thread and arrange the gathers evenly. Tack down securely where the two rows meet in the center.

6 Take the 24" (61cm) length of 2"-wide (5cm-wide) ribbon, and fold it over width-wise, enclosing the dull side of the ribbon. Measure out six 4" (10cm) sections along the doubled length, marking each with pins. Using double threads, stitch the following pattern for multiple petals through the two layers of ribbon, gathering as you do each section. Make sure your thread loops over the top of the folded edge each time you go up and angle down the other side of the pins. Keep an eye on the bottom layer, taking care that you are catching it as well.

Draw up all the gathers and measure to fit around the first two rows as before (sometimes you have to spread them back out a little). Knot off and arrange them evenly. Tack them down securely where they meet the previous row.

7 The outer row has five large petals. Take the 40" (102cm) length of ribbon and measure five 8" (20cm) sections along the length. Mark these with pins. This section is sewn like the previous row, except you do not fold the ribbon. Start the stitches on the outside selvedge, just in from the raw edge, and stitch as before for multiple petals. Don't forget to gather as you go. Once finished, wrap the new section around the base of the three inner rows, arrange the petals evenly, and knot off the threads. Tack securely to the previous row and carefully trim away the excess crinoline underneath.

Each row is tacked around the previous row on the crinoline.

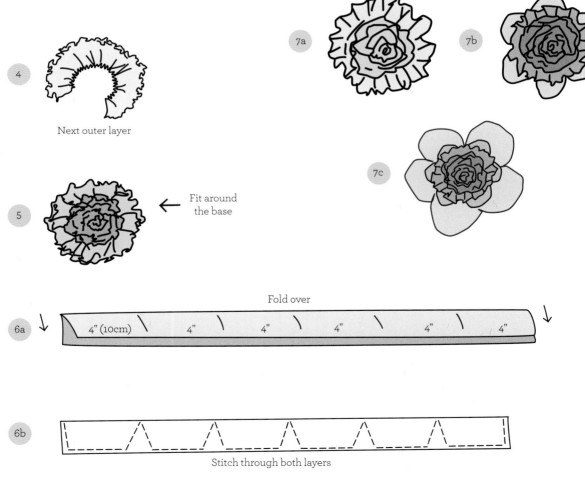

4 — Next outer layer

5 — Fit around the base

6a — Fold over — 4" (10cm) 4" 4" 4" 4" 4"

7a

7b

7c

6b — Stitch through both layers

Create a Fragrant Sachet

Perfect for a drawer or closet, the addition of the peony makes this sachet lovely enough to display out in the open where it can be admired.

materials

1 Peony ribbon flower

12" (30cm) of 6"-wide (15cm-wide) ribbon (any type you prefer)

Dried lavender

Pin back (optional)

Matching thread

Scissors

Needle

1. Make the Peony ribbon flower. Add a pin back if you want it to be removable.

2. Take the 12" (30cm) of ribbon and cut it in half so you have two 6" (15cm) squares. Place the squares with their right sides facing each other and stitch them together. Leave a 3" (8cm) opening.

3. Turn the stitched sachet body right side out. Make sure you turn out the corners; use chopsticks or a knitting needle to make them point out correctly.

4. Fill your sachet pillow with the lavender.

5. Stitch up the opening with small stitches to seal in the lavender.

6. Pin or hand tack the Peony to the top of your sachet pillow.

PETAL FLOWER

This simple flower can be made singly or with the two sizes stacked together to form a rosette. You can use a jewel or button for the center, or stamens. Most ribbon, wired or unwired, works for this flower.

materials

12½" (32cm) of 1"-wide (3cm-wide) ribbon for a medium blossom

18¾" (48cm) of 1½"-wide (4cm-wide) ribbon for a large blossom

Matching thread

Stamens (optional)

Jewels or buttons (optional)

Needle

If using wired taffeta, remove the wire from the selvedge that you want to be the inside of the flower, leaving the selvedge wire intact for the petal edges.

1 Take the ribbon and divide it into five equal sections. You can do this by making five folds and pressing each fold to make a crease. You can also use straight pins to mark each section. For 1"-wide (3cm-wide) ribbon, these sections will be 2½" (6cm) each. For the 2"-wide (5cm-wide) ribbon, these sections will be 3¾" (10cm) each.

2 Take a double-threaded needle and start a knot on the selvedge of the ribbon that will be the outside edge of the petals. Do this just in from the raw edge. Follow the stitch pattern below, looping your thread over the wired selvedge as you stitch up and back down again. Gather slightly as you go along; this makes it much easier to pull all the gathers once the stitching is completed.

3 Gather all the stitched sections and knot the thread to hold, leaving your needle and thread attached. Use the needle and thread to tack the two ends of the flower together to make it circular. Tack only in the center where both of your knots are, turning them to the back of the flower. Once you have finished the flower, you can add your center. If the opening in the middle of the flower is too large, reduce its size with extra stitches.

4 For stamens, take a double-threaded needle and lay it on your work surface with the threads out in a straight line. Take eighteen to twenty stamens and lay them in a bundle across the end of the thread. Tie the thread securely around the center of the stamen stems. It's a good idea to wrap the thread several times and then knot once more to hold them securely. Fold the stamens in half at the juncture of your thread so they hang off the end of your thread, much like a fishing lure.

5 Place the stamens in the center opening of the flower and stitch the center closed around them, pulling the threads taught and going through the bundle of stamens as you stitch. Knot off securely to hold.

6 For a rosette shape, make a Petal Flower of each size. Tack the small flower to the center of the large flower. Add stamens or another embellishment for the center.

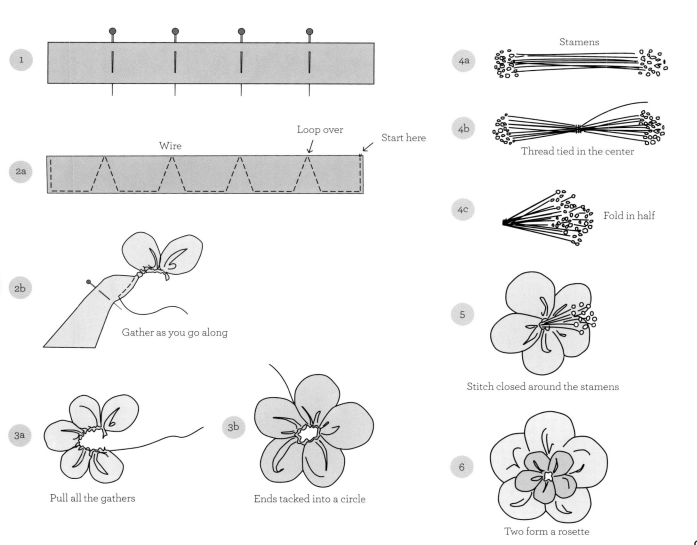

Stamens

Thread tied in the center

Fold in half

Wire

Loop over

Start here

Gather as you go along

Pull all the gathers

Ends tacked into a circle

Stitch closed around the stamens

Two form a rosette

PLEATED JEWELED ROSETTE

These delicate creations are about as elegant as you can get with ribbon. When affixed to a hat or lapel, the effect is exquisite. Due to the water technique used in their creation, bias-cut silk ribbon works best for these rosettes.

materials

½ yd. (46cm) of 1"-wide (3cm-wide) silk ribbon for a small rosette

or

1 yd. (.9cm) of 1½"-wide (4cm-wide) silk ribbon for a large rosette

Matching jewel or button for the center

Matching thread

Crinoline

Needle

Waterproof work surface

Paper towels

When working with wet ribbons, be aware that the color can sometimes transfer to other materials.

1 Begin by thoroughly wetting the length of ribbon under cold water. Don't wring it out and transfer it, still dripping, to your waterproof work surface. You can keep a cold bowl of water on your work area or transfer the ribbon from the sink on a saucer. To make a waterproof surface, lay a piece of plastic on your table or use a medium to large water- and stainproof tray to work on.

2 Start at one end of the ribbon and begin pleating it tightly with your fingers. It's best to leave the ribbon lying flat on your surface for this. Work your way along the ribbon, occasionally scrunching the accumulated pleats together on the work surface, until it is completely pleated. Don't try to make the pleats perfectly even; you won't be able to, and it's best if the pleats are uneven, even somewhat crinkled. By now the ribbon will be a fraction of its original size.

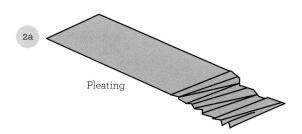

2a Pleating

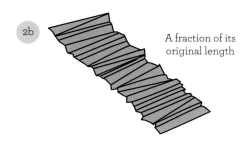

2b A fraction of its original length

3 Once the pleats are finished, take several layers of paper towels and lay the bundle of pleated ribbon on top, taking care not to undo the pleats. Tightly roll the pleated bundle up in the paper towels to blot any water and dye that may come out. Squeeze the bundle tightly to set the pleats even more. Unroll the paper towels and remove the ribbon. Thoroughly clean your work surface with a cleaning spray to avoid any dye residue and dry it off.

Carefully open the pleated ribbon, stretching it out about 12" (30cm), and lay it out to dry. This can take anywhere from twenty minutes to half an hour if the weather is not humid.

4 When your ribbon is totally dry, the pleats will be set, so you can work with it freely. Take a double-threaded needle and start a knot on one selvedge, just in from the raw edge. Do this on the selvedge of the ribbon you want to show on the outer edge of your rosette. Start a gathering stitch down the raw edge to the opposite selvedge, and then turn along it, stitching the entire length of the ribbon and back up to the opposite side. Gather as you go along, following the stitch pattern shown.

5 Once you have finished stitching, pull all the gathers and knot the thread securely. If your ribbon has a right side, turn it facing up and overlap one end over the other, turning any visible raw edges under. Tack the two layers together in the center to form the circular rosette.

6 Once the rosette is stitched in its circular form, securely tack it down to a 4" (10cm) circle of crinoline using a double-threaded needle. Tack only in the center; leave the pleats free. Once you have attached the rosette to the crinoline, you can add the center jewel by sewing or gluing it in, then adding one or two stitches to secure it. To finish, carefully trim away the crinoline.

Stretch out slightly to dry

3

4 ← Start here

Stitch through the pleats

5 Tack into a rosette

6 Add center

Create a French Bulletin Board

When hung on the wall or displayed on an easel, this bulletin board assumes the status of art. The ribbons allow you to tuck in photos and keepsakes you don't want to put a pushpin in.

materials

9 small Pleated Jeweled Rosettes (or your favorite ribbon flower)

One 24" × 36" (61cm × 91cm) corkboard with wood frame

1⅛ yds. (103cm) of fabric

8 yds. (7.3m) of ⅜"-wide (10mm-wide) or ⅝"-wide (16mm-wide) ribbon

Hot glue gun

Glue sticks

Decorative upholstery tacks

Staple gun

1 Lay the fabric face down and place the bulletin board on top the fabric. Trim the fabric so that all four sides have 2½" (6cm) of fabric overhanging.

2 Starting at the top of the board, begin folding over the fabric. Work from the center out toward one side, then the other. Staple the fabric down as you go, placing the staples about 1" to 2" (3cm to 5cm) apart. When you get to the corner of the bulletin board, leave about 2" (5cm) unstapled.

3 Do the bottom of the board in the same manner. Make sure your fabric is pulled taut as you staple.

4 Repeat the process for each of the two sides.

5 To finish the corners, pull the fabric taut on each corner and staple. Trim off the extra fabric, then staple the remaining 2" (5cm) on each of the sides.

6 Turn your bulletin board face up. Start at one corner and lay out the ribbon on the diagonal to the opposite corner. Add more rows in the same direction, spacing the ribbon about 9" (23cm) apart as you go.

7 Repeat the layout for your ribbon in the opposite direction.

8 Secure the ribbons at each intersection with an upholstery tack.

9 Staple or hot glue all of the ribbon ends to the back of the bulletin board. Trim off any excess ribbon.

10 Hot glue the flowers to every other row of ribbon intersections (or to every intersection if you prefer).

POINSETTIA

Poinsettias originated in Mexico and are the classic holiday flower we think of when Christmas comes to mind. They have been hybridized to create a variety of colors beyond the classic red and white, including yellow, peach and multicolored. Use wired taffeta for these easy-to-make beauties that look gorgeous on a wreath, a package or even a lapel.

materials

2¼ yds. (2m) of 1"-wide (3cm-wide) wired taffeta ribbon for a small Poinsettia

or

1 yd. (.9m) of 1"-wide (3cm-wide) wired taffeta ribbon and 1⅞ yds. (1.7m) of 1½"-wide (4cm-wide) wired taffeta ribbon for a medium Poinsettia

Poinsettia stamens

Matching thread

Crinoline

Needle

cutting

Outer petals: Cut the 1½"-wide (4cm-wide) ribbon into five 13" (33cm) lengths

Inner petals: Cut the 1"-wide (3cm-wide) ribbon into three 10" (25cm) lengths

1. Make all the petals using the same instructions for the Basic Leaf. Five will be the outer petals, and the remaining three will be the inner petals. For the small Poinsettia, cut eight 10" (25cm) lengths for all the petals. For a medium Poinsettia, cut the 1½"-wide (4cm-wide) ribbon into five 13" (33cm) lengths for the outer petals, and cut the 1"-wide (3cm-wide) ribbon into three 10" (25cm) lengths for the inner petals. Use the stitch pattern below to create each petal.

2. Once all the petals are completed, tack the outer row of petals into a circle on a 4" × 4" (10cm × 10cm) square of crinoline with their sides touching. Tack from underneath and toward the center, allowing the outer points to be free of stitches.

3. Take eight to ten Poinsettia stamens and fold them in half. Tack them securely to the crinoline in the center of the ring of outer petals. Make sure they stand up by tacking the folded ends tightly to the crinoline in an upright position.

4. Take the inner set of petals and tack them around the stamens, completely covering the center. Try to get the points of the inner petals between the points of two of the outer petals to avoid too much overlapping. Pull the inner petals close around the stamens and tack strategically to hold them in place.

5. Trim away the crinoline and arrange the petal points as needed.

Basic leaf stitch pattern

5 petals

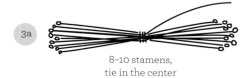

8–10 stamens,
tie in the center

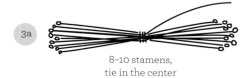

Fold and tack upright

Stamens in the center

Final 3 petals

The secret to this flower is that all of the petals are made exactly like the Basic Leaf. You will have an outer row of five petals and an inner row of three petals.

POM-POM FLOWER

This striking design is both flirty and unique. There is no limit to color choice, but be sure to use bias-cut silk ribbon to get just the right look for this ribbon creation.

materials

1½ yds. (1.4cm) of 2½"-wide (6cm-wide) silk ribbon

Matching thread

Crinoline

Needle

1 Take the ribbon and fray along both selvedges with the blade of your scissors (much like you would curl ribbon for gifts). You want a nice, fuzzy edge on both selvedges. Don't fret if you create a few tears—they won't be noticed.

2 Lay out the frayed ribbon and measure one-third of the way down from the edge you want to show in the center of the flower. Create a seamline by creasing down the length of the ribbon with a fingernail.

3 Fold the ribbon over on itself, wrong side to wrong side, to make a French seam. Sew the two raw ends together with small stitches and a ¼" (6mm) seam allowance, making the length of ribbon into a big loop. You want to enclose the seam, so turn the ribbon inside out and lay it flat to make it right side to right side. Make another row of stitches along ¼" from the folded seam to enclose the raw edge. Take care to keep the stitches neat and small. Turn the ribbon inside out once more.

4 Start a knot on the crease you created one-third of the way down from the top. Put your knot right on the seam. Start stitching the circumference of the ribbon, gathering as you go. When you have come fully around to where you started, pull all the gathers and knot off securely.

5 Flatten the gathered piece, making sure the wide part of the ribbon is on the bottom and the one-third on top in the middle. Check to make sure all of the top is pulled up through the hole in your gathered center. Take it up and stitch back and forth though the center a few times to pull it closed more tightly, and flatten it out once more.

6 Take a 4" × 4" (10cm × 10cm) square of crinoline and tack the Pom-Pom Flower down, keeping the stitches at the center. Trim away the excess crinoline and fluff the center, if needed.

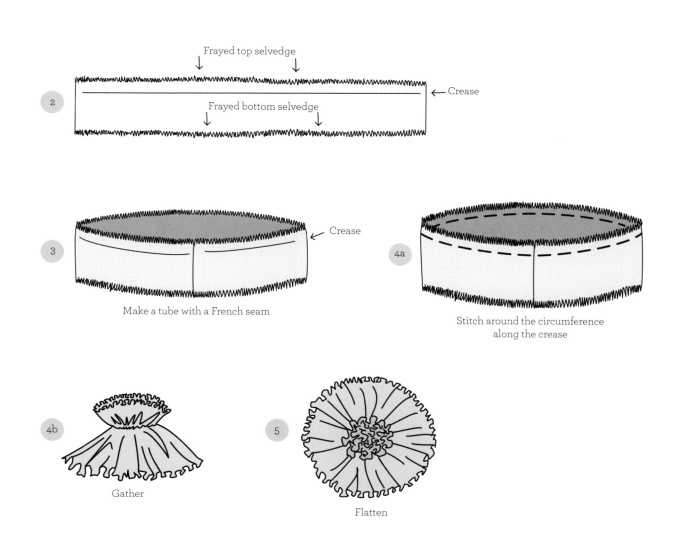

2 — Frayed top selvedge
← Crease
Frayed bottom selvedge

3 — Crease
Make a tube with a French seam

4a — Stitch around the circumference along the crease

4b — Gather

5 — Flatten

POPPY

Poppies: delicate, mysterious and intoxicating, these flowers have always enchanted. Use taffeta ribbon for these flowers in the classic red; you can also make them in brilliant orange, yellow, white or pink.

materials

1 yd. (.9m) of 1½"-wide (4cm-wide) wired taffeta ribbon for the petals

9" (23cm) of ⅝"- or ½"-wide (16mm or 13mm-wide) wired taffeta for the ruffle under the berry

6" (15cm) of 1"-wide (3cm-wide) wired taffeta ribbon for the center berry

25–30 stamens, black for the classic Poppy or bright green for the Icelandic Poppy

Crinoline

Matching thread

Medium-size cotton balls

Needle

1   Start with the 1 yard (.9m) length of ribbon and remove the wire on the edge of the selvedge that will be the inside of the petals. Leave the wire for the outer edge of the petals intact. Cut the length into four 9" (23cm) pieces. Take one of the cut lengths and make a knot using a double-threaded needle on the top right wired selvedge, ¼" (6mm) from the raw edge. These petals are made one at a time, using the single-petal stitch pattern shown.

Gather tightly and knot the thread, crinkling the wired edges with your fingers. Make all four petals in the same manner.

2   Once the petals are made, tack the first two to the crinoline opposite one another, leaving about ¼" (6mm) between the two. Tack only in the center in the gathered areas. Take the other two petals and tack these across the first two on opposite sides. Allow the same amount of space between them. Tack through both layers at the center, and knot off the thread on the back.

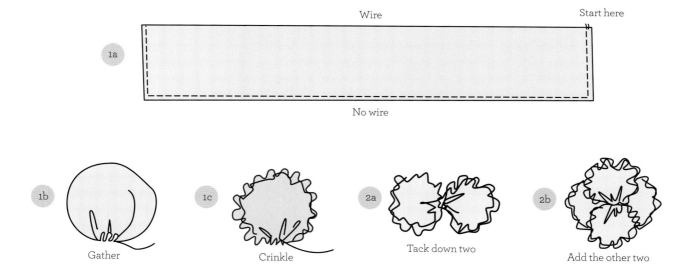

1a   Wire   Start here   No wire

1b Gather   1c Crinkle   2a Tack down two   2b Add the other two

3 Take the 9" (23cm) length of ⅝"-wide (16mm-wide) or ½"-wide (13mm-wide) ribbon and remove one of the wires. Make a rosette by following the stitch pattern shown, drawing up tightly and knotting off. Overlap one end over the other and tack to hold, creating the rosette. Pleat around the circumference on the wired edge.

4 Take the stamens in groups of two or three and lay them across the rosette. Tack them down in the center so the heads hang out over the edge of the rosette. Crisscross them so the rosette is evenly covered with stamens. Tack this finished piece into the center of your petals.

5 Remove both wires from the 6" (15cm) length of ribbon and stitch the two raw ends together using small, close stitches to make a tube. Leave a ¼" (6mm) seam allowance and don't gather the ribbon. Knot off the thread and turn the ribbon inside out, leaving your needle and thread intact. Stitch around the circumference of one selvedge, which will be the top, as this center berry is stuffed with cotton from the bottom. Stitch all the way around to the beginning. Pull these stitches tightly and knot the thread on the inside, clipping away the needle.

6 Stitch along the other selvedge in the same manner. When you've stitched all the way around, begin to draw up the stitches while stuffing the inside with cotton a bit at a time. It takes about one medium cotton ball, sometimes one and a half, to stuff the center berry firmly. Draw the stitches closed around the berry and knot the thread securely, leaving the needle and thread attached.

7 Take the needle with the berry still on it and run it through the middle of the rosette of stamens, pulling it firmly into the center. Come up from underneath the berry and tack it securely in place by angling into the bottom with the needle as you go back down and up. Tack around the bottom of the berry in this fashion. Once it is secure, trim away the crinoline. Lightly pinch the edges of the petals to create soft crinkles and give them a realistic look.

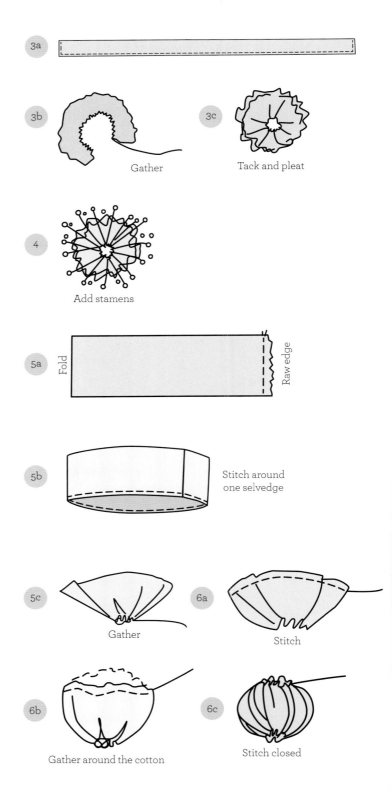

3a

3b
Gather

3c
Tack and pleat

4
Add stamens

5a
Fold
Raw edge

5b
Stitch around one selvedge

5c
Gather

6a
Stitch

6b
Gather around the cotton

6c
Stitch closed

PULLED WIRE ROSE

This simple-to-create and elegant flower has been around for while. Early versions were found on dresses, gowns, and hats during the Roaring Twenties and the Belle Époque. Today these are gathered on the wire using the wonderful variety of wired ribbons available. Ombre and variegated ribbons make striking rosettes, but patterned ribbons turn out beautiful examples as well.

materials

Wired taffeta :

- If using ⅝"-wide (16mm-wide) ribbon, cut ½ yd. (46cm)

- If using 1"-wide (3cm-wide) ribbon, cut 1 yd. (.9m)

- If using 1½"-wide (4cm-wide) ribbon, cut 2 yds. (1.8m)

- If using 2"-wide (5cm-wide) or 3"-wide (8cm-wide) ribbon, cut 2½ yds. (2.3m) or more

Matching thread

Needle

If your wire breaks during gathering, simply push the remaining end of the wire out of the selvedge and continue gathering from that point. Clip away all but ¾" (19mm) of the wire and fold it over on itself to hold it momentarily. Using a double-threaded needle, start a knot on the selvedge, enclosing the wire to secure it. Start stitching back up the length of the ribbon where wire broke, then gather it. Knot the thread, clip away the needle and thread, and proceed to make the rose as shown.

1. Take the length of ribbon and tie a knot in one end. This will serve as the center underneath, which you will coil the gathered ribbon around.

2. Decide which wired edge will be the inner part of the rosette. The ungathered edge will be the outer, and most visible, part of the flower. Start gathering the ribbon along the wire, gently pushing and pulling the gathers toward the knotted end. Continue to gather until you can no longer move the ribbon along the wire.

   Once you have gathered the ribbon, pull out about 1" (3cm) of the wire on the ungathered side and twist both wires together securely to hold the gathers. Don't cut away the exposed wire before securing, as sometimes the ribbon can slide up the wire. Twist tightly and cut away the excess wire, leaving about ½" (13mm) remaining.

3. Start coiling the gathers around the knot to form the rosette, keeping the knot exposed underneath. Don't allow the selvedges to overlap, but let them spiral out from the knot instead. The rosette will more or less hold its shape, but pins can be used to secure it before tacking.

4. Once the rosette is formed, begin tacking on the underside using double threads. Tack the rows of selvedges to one another starting in the center and working outward. Don't pull the thread too tightly; the key is to tack, not to stitch. The raw edge with the exposed wire can be folded toward the center knot and tacked down. Finish by turning the rosette to the front and arranging the ribbon.

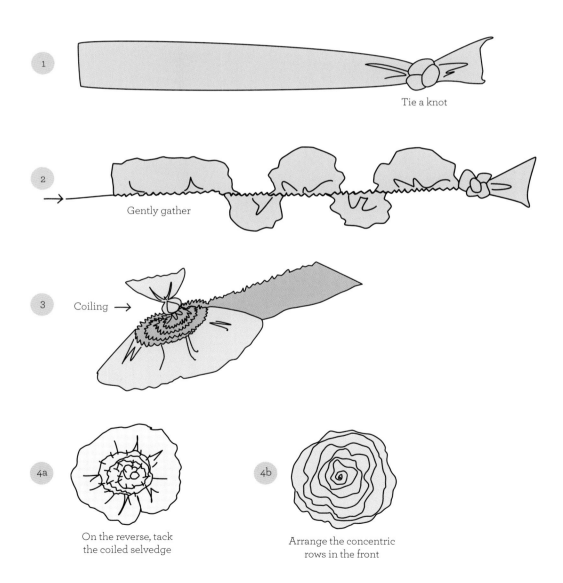

1   Tie a knot

2   Gently gather

3   Coiling →

4a   On the reverse, tack the coiled selvedge

4b   Arrange the concentric rows in the front

VARIATION: CRINKLED ROSE

The Crinkled Rose is a variation of the Pulled Wire Rose. It is made in the same fashion as the Pulled Wire Rose, with the exception of crinkling the ribbon beforehand. This extra step adds a new dimension to the flower, giving it a crushed, vintage look. Use wired taffeta for this rose, and don't be afraid to really crush the ribbon!

materials

Wired taffeta :

- If using ⅝"-wide (16mm-wide) ribbon, cut ½ yd. (46cm)

- If using 1"-wide (3cm-wide) ribbon, cut 1 yd. (.9m)

- If using 1½-wide" (4cm-wide) ribbon cut 2 yds. (1.8m)

- If using 2"-wide (5cm-wide) or 3"-wide (8cm-wide) ribbon cut 2½ yds. (2.3m) or more

Matching thread

Needle

1 Begin by plunging the entire length of ribbon into a bowl of cold water. Alternatively, you can fold it loosely and hold it under cold running water to thoroughly wet it.

2 Lay the wet ribbon on a waterproof surface. Flatten the ribbon in front of you and begin scrunching it up tightly, bit by bit, from one end. Work your way down the length of the ribbon, crinkling it and allowing the water to seep out. When you have crinkled the entire length of the ribbon, take it in your hands and crush it tightly into a ball, squeezing out any remaining water.

Once you have given it a final squeeze, gently tease open the ball of ribbon and stretch it out loosely. The length will be about half of what it was at the start. Allow the ribbon to dry thoroughly before continuing.

3 To complete the Crinkled Rose, follow steps 1–4 of the Pulled Wire Rose.

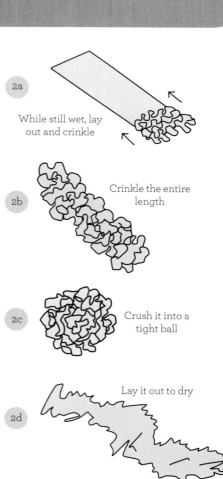

2a While still wet, lay out and crinkle

2b Crinkle the entire length

2c Crush it into a tight ball

2d Lay it out to dry

VARIATION: PLEATED ROSE

The Pleated Rose is another variation of the Pulled Wire Rose. Like the Crinkled Rose, it is made in the same fashion as the Pulled Wire Rose, with the exception that it is pleated when wet rather than crinkled. Use wired taffeta for this rose and keep in mind that the more tightly you press the pleats into the ribbon, the more crisp they will be when dry.

materials

Wired taffeta:

- If using ⅝"-wide (16mm-wide) ribbon, cut ½ yd. (46cm)

- If using 1"-wide (3cm-wide) ribbon, cut 1 yd. (.9m)

- If using 1½"-wide (4cm-wide) ribbon, cut 2 yds. (1.8m)

- If using 2"-wide (5cm-wide) or 3"-wide (8cm-wide) ribbon, cut 2½ yds. (2.3m) or more

Matching thread

Needle

1   Begin by thoroughly wetting the length of ribbon under cold water. Don't wring it out and transfer it to a waterproof surface.

2   Begin pleating from one end of the ribbon by creasing it tightly into ¼" (6mm) pleats with your fingers. It's best to leave the ribbon lying flat on your surface for this. Work your way along the ribbon, occasionally scrunching the accumulated pleats together. Don't worry about making the pleats perfectly even. By now the ribbon will be a fraction of its original size.

3   Once the pleats are finished, take several layers of paper towels and lay the bundle of pleated ribbon on top, taking care not to undo the pleats. Tightly roll the pleated bundle up in the paper towels to blot out any excess water and dye. Unroll the paper towels and remove the ribbon. Thoroughly clean your work surface with a cleaning spray to avoid any dye residue.

4   Carefully open the pleated ribbon, stretching it out about 12" (30cm), and lay it out to dry. This can take anywhere from twenty minutes to half an hour if the weather is not humid.

5   When your ribbon is totally dry, the pleats will be set, and you can work with it freely. To complete the Pleated Rose, follow steps 1–4 of the Pulled Wire Rose.

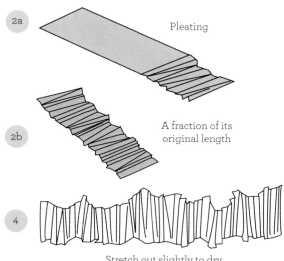

2a Pleating

2b A fraction of its original length

4   Stretch out slightly to dry

RIBBON MEDALLION

The Ribbon Medallion is one of the most elegant of the ribbon adornments. Its style echoes the eighteenth century and the sort of embellishment one might find on a luxurious gown worn by Marie Antoinette. It's very easy to create, and you can use most types of ribbon.

materials

20" (51cm) of 1½"-wide (4cm-wide) satin or wired taffeta

Jeweled button or other similar item for the center (you can also use a small brooch)

Matching thread

Needle

The medallion is fashioned from cut lengths of folded ribbon (like petals) gathered at the bottom and tacked in a circle. The center jewel is then added. Don't hesitate to experiment with different lengths and types of ribbon for this embellishment.

1 Cut five 4" (10cm) lengths of ribbon and fold each one in half lengthwise.

2 Tack two pleats into the bottom raw edges of each piece by folding the selvedges next to the raw edges in toward each other. Tack them securely to hold. Alternatively, you can stitch across the bottom raw edge and simply gather, knotting off the thread to hold. Make all five petals in this manner before continuing to the next step.

3 Take a 4" × 4" (10cm × 10cm) square of crinoline with the corners rounded, and pin the five medallion petals in a circle with the sides touching. Arrange them evenly. Once you are satisfied with the arrangement, tack the medallion petals down, keeping your stitches at the center. When you have secured them, add a center jewel or button.

Carefully trim away the excess crinoline underneath and pouf up the medallion petals with your fingers.

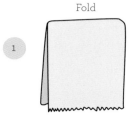

Fold

1

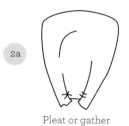

2a

Pleat or gather

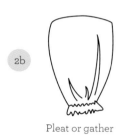

2b

Pleat or gather

3a

Tack the petals into a rosette

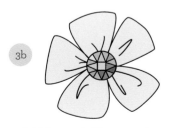

3b

Add the jeweled button to the center

RUFFLE COCKADE

The classic Ruffle Cockade is the simplest of all the cockades to make. Grosgrain ribbon works best, but you can also use satin, taffeta and silk.

materials

The amount of ribbon used for this cockade can vary due to the different thicknesses of various ribbons. The following measurements work best:

1 yd. (.9m) of 1"-wide (3cm-wide) ribbon for a small cockade

1¼ yds. (1.1m) of 1½"-wide (4cm-wide) ribbon for a medium cockade

1½ yds. (1.4m) of 2"-wide (5cm-wide) or wider ribbon for a large cockade

Matching thread

Needle

Jewel or button (optional)

The Ruffle Cockade is made by creating twenty-five folds in a zigzag pattern that are tacked together in the center. The folds are one-third the width of the ribbon being used. For a thicker cockade, you can make the folds half the width of the ribbon but add ¼ yard (23cm) to the length being used. Use a double-threaded needle for making this cockade.

1. Lay your ribbon out flat and measure 1" (3cm) from one end and mark with a pin. Measuring lengthwise from the previous pin, place a second pin at a distance about a third of the ribbon's width.

2. Take the ribbon and fold it over from the second pin toward the first. This creates your first fold. Tack the ribbon together on the top selvedge at the first pin, and then move your needle over to tack the fold at the second pin. As you make more folds, you will continue to tack the folds in these two places, moving your needle from one side to the other. Tack twice each time to hold.

3. Remove the pins. Take the ribbon up and use your fingers to make another fold over the first one in a zigzag formation. Keep the edges straight and make sure the fold is the same length as the first one. Tack the fold to the previous one at each side of the selvedge, as before. Press the folds tightly with your fingers to keep them crisp and together.

4. Create twenty-five folds in this manner, tacking and pressing as you go. If you run out of thread, simply knot the original thread securely and start a fresh knot with your new thread on the next fold and continue.

5. When you have created all of your folds, bring the two ends of the folds together. Each end will have a tail, which will hang under the cockade. Tack each side together where the tails meet, making sure they meet evenly to close the folds into a circle. Trim the excess ribbon on the tails to about ½" (13mm) to allow you to stitch them together properly.

6. Starting from the center, stitch the two tails together below the edges of the folds to complete the cockade. Knot the thread discreetly on the outside selvedge and cut away the needle and thread. Carefully trim away the remaining bit of the tails that extend past the bottom folds. Turn the cockade over to the front and arrange the pleats, adding a center, if desired.

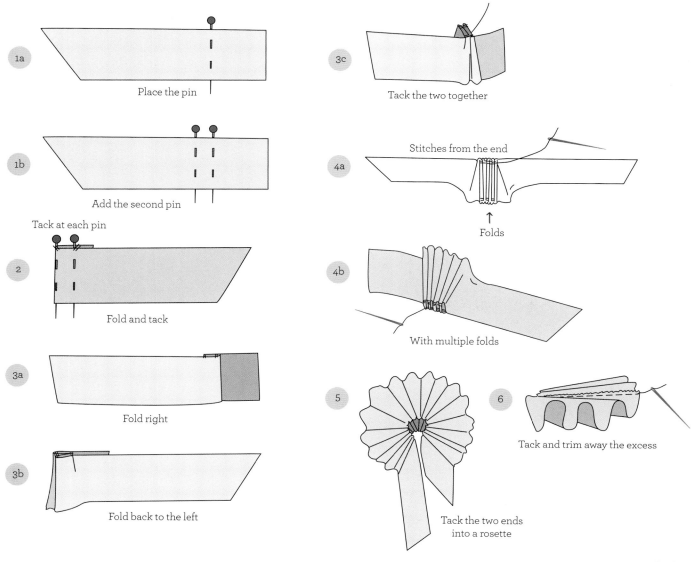

1a — Place the pin

1b — Add the second pin

2 — Tack at each pin / Fold and tack

3a — Fold right

3b — Fold back to the left

3c — Tack the two together

4a — Stitches from the end / Folds

4b — With multiple folds

5 — Tack the two ends into a rosette

6 — Tack and trim away the excess

SILK FOLDED ROSE

This is a very easy ribbon rose to make. Bias-cut silk ribbon is essential for achieving the right look for this simple, yet elegant creation.

materials

2 yds. (1.8m) of 2"-wide (5cm-wide) bias-cut silk ribbon

Matching thread

Needle

1 Lay out the ribbon, and fold it widthwise, taking care to enclose the ribbon's dull side, if it has one. Secure with pins so you can stitch through both layers easily. Thread a needle with double threads at about 25" (64cm).

2 Place a knot on the fold just in from one raw edge and stitch the pattern below. Take care to catch both layers and gather as you go along.

3 Once you have stitched the length of the ribbon, lay it out and gather it to a final length of about 19"–20" (48cm–51cm), turning all the ruffles to one side. When you have reached this length, knot the thread securely. The next step is to rearrange the gathers. This is important, as the distribution of gathers determines the final shape of the flower.

4 Start at one end of the ribbon and spread the gathers out thinly, allowing them to get thicker as you move down the length of the ribbon. Make the transition as gradual as possible so there isn't a sudden clump of gathered area next to a thinly gathered area. The thinly gathered part of the ribbon will be the center, so you'll need to coil this section more tightly than the rest of the ribbon.

5 Once you have arranged the gathers, begin rolling up the ribbon, starting with three full turns. Tack at the bottom as you go along to hold the rolls in place, then roll in half-turns and tack. Make sure the bottom of the rolled gathers remain even with one another. With silk, it's easy to let the tacked area underneath slide and become concave or convex. This causes the center on the front of the flower to either pop up too high or sink down too low. Roll as evenly as possible, holding the bottom of the gathers firmly in your hand.

Once you've finished rolling and tacking, check the front to see if you need to pull the center in with a few stitches, then knot off to hold.

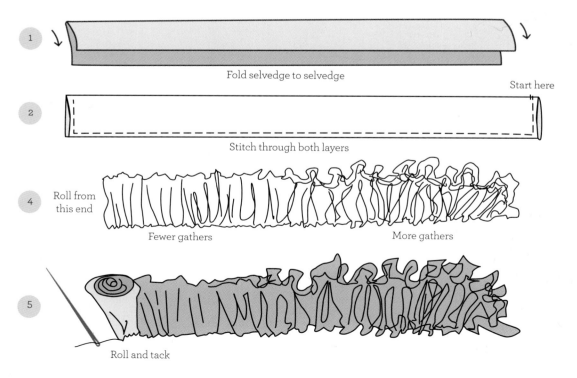

1 Fold selvedge to selvedge

Start here

2 Stitch through both layers

4 Roll from this end

Fewer gathers   More gathers

5 Roll and tack

Create an Elegant Headband

The burnt coque feathers add a flirty hint to this easily made headband. If you don't have burnt coque, you can use regular feathers in their place.

materials

2 Silk Folded Roses (or flowers of your choice)

Headband

Feather pad

Burnt coque feathers

Hot glue gun

Glue sticks

Velvet leaves

1 Glue the feather pad to the headband.

2 Arrange the burnt coque feathers as desired and glue them to the back of the ribbon flower.

3 Position and glue the ribbon flowers and feathers to the feather pad and headband.

4 Glue the velvet leaves to the reverse of the pad and flowers to additionally secure them from the inside of the headband.

TEA ROSE

The Tea Rose is a culmination of centuries of hybridization by growers the world over. These blooms are unfailingly fragrant, large-bloomed beauties that reign queen-like over any garden. Tea Roses come in an astonishing array of colors as well. This ribbon version is a faithful reproduction of the Tea Rose and is made with wired taffeta. You can use a solid, iridescent, ombre or variegated ribbon for these beauties.

materials

½ yd. (46m) of 1"-wide (3cm-wide) wired taffeta for the inner petals

1¼ yds. (1.1m) of 1½"-wide (4cm-wide) taffeta for the middle and outer rows of petals

Matching stamens

Matching thread

Crinoline

Needle-nose pliers or tweezers (chopsticks or knitting needles will work as well)

Needle

The Tea Rose is made up of three sections of petals around a central grouping of stamens. It's best to make all the petals before assembling the flower. The easiest way to start is to cut all the lengths of ribbon for the three rows of petals and lay them out in stacks according to size on your work surface.

For the inner petals, cut six 3" (8cm) lengths of the 1"-wide (3cm-wide) ribbon and remove all the wires.

For the middle section of petals, cut five 3½" (9cm) lengths of the 1½"-wide (4cm-wide) ribbon, leaving all the wires intact.

For the outer row of petals, cut six 4" (10cm) lengths of the 1½"-wide (4cm-wide) ribbon, leaving all the wires intact.

1 Cut your ribbon to the correct lengths for the petals as instructed above. Take one of the 3" (8cm) lengths of unwired ribbon and make a single gathered petal using the stitch pattern shown. Start a knot on the outside selvedge of the ribbon. This will be the petal edge that shows. Stitch down along the raw edge, along the bottom selvedge and up the opposite raw edge. Gather the ribbon tightly before knotting off the thread. Complete all six petals in this manner before moving to the next step.

2 Once you have completed all the inner petals, assemble them around the stamens. Take a double-threaded needle and lay it on your work surface with the thread out in a straight line. Take about eighteen to twenty stamens and lay them in a bundle across the end of the thread. Tie the thread securely around the center of the stamen stems. Wrap the thread several times, then knot once more to hold them securely. Fold the stamens in half at the juncture of your thread so they hang off the end of your thread, much like a fishing lure.

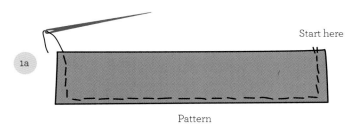

Start here

1a

Pattern

Gathered petal

1b

Lay out stamens

2a

Tie thread in center

Fold down

2b

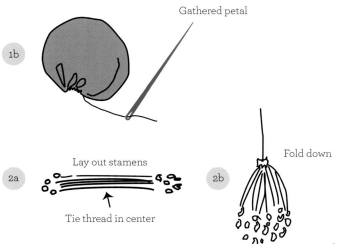

3 Tack the petals one by one around the folded bottom of the bundle. Begin with two across from each other. Carefully work your needle through the knot and stamens and tack the bottom where they join together. Allow the petal edges to overlap one another. The next two petals are tacked evenly around these two; the third is set evenly around those, forming a rosette. Knot your thread when all six are securely tacked around the stamens, and lay it aside to make the next set of petals.

4 The middle and outer row of petals are both made by rolling or folding the wired corners to shape the petals. You will be working from what will be the back of the petal.

Start with the five 3½" (9cm) lengths of ribbon for the middle row. Fold each one in half lengthwise. Take the needle-nose pliers or tweezers and roll one of the folded corners over twice, about ⅛" (3mm) each time. Use a double-threaded needle to tack the fold to the layer it is folded onto, avoiding the bottom layer of ribbon, which is actually the front of the petal. Check to see that you haven't gone through the other layer before you knot off and clip away the thread. If you'd like to hide your knot and threads better, you can also hold the two petal layers open and start your needle from between the layers, then knot off on the inside and clip away the threads. Roll and tack the opposite corner in the same fashion.

5 Turn the petal over to the front and pleat both sides at the bottom by taking each edge and lifting it over on itself to make a pleat. This is not a fold, but a pleat, so the edge remains the edge, but it is angled toward the bottom. Tack each pleat securely. Doing each edge of the petal like this gives it a realistic pucker. Complete the other four petals in this manner before moving on to the outer row.

For the outer row of petals, take the 4" (10cm) lengths of ribbon and fold them in half lengthwise as before. Make each of these longer petals in the same manner as the previous row.

6 When you have completed all three sets of petals, the Tea Rose is ready to assemble. On a 4" (10cm) circle of crinoline, pin the outer row of larger petals in a circle so their edges overlap slightly. The crinoline will show through in the center. Once you have the petals arranged evenly in a circle, tack each one securely to the crinoline with double thread. Do this at the bottom of each petal where the pleats are, leaving the length of the petal free. Remove the pins as you tack each petal and make adjustments along the way.

7 When you have completed the outer row, pin the middle row of petals in place in a circle over those. Allow them to overlap slightly, making the center hole smaller. Tack these down as you did the outer row, going through all the layers securely.

8 To finish the Tea Rose, tack the inner set of petals with the stamens securely to the center of the two outer rows of petals. Tack securely at the base, going around the bottom circumference and through all the layers. If there are any gaps between the inner and middle rows of petals, pull them together with tight stitches, knotting off securely on the underside. Trim away the excess crinoline, and arrange the stamens by lightly pinching them with your fingers and turning them slightly while pushing down. Spread them open and adjust the petals.

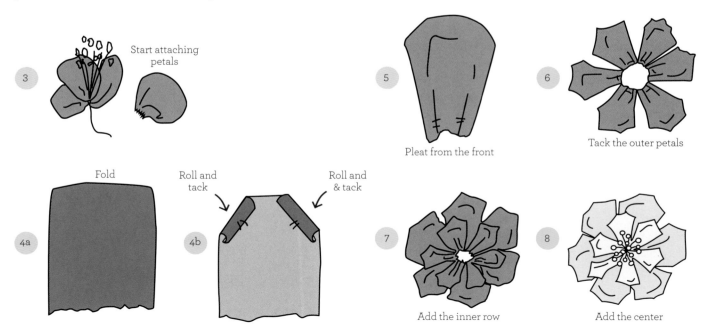

3 Start attaching petals

Fold 4a

Roll and tack · Roll and & tack 4b

5 Pleat from the front

6 Tack the outer petals

7 Add the inner row

8 Add the center

RESOURCES

The following is a list of the excellent resources used to create the projects in this book:

NICHOLAS KNIEL

Fine Ribbon & Embellishments

290 Hilderbrand Drive B-13
Atlanta, GA 30328
404-252-8855
www.NicholasKniel.com

All of the ribbons featured in this book can be found at Nicholas Kniel Fine Ribbons & Embellishments. We also carry buttons, crystal appliqués, crinoline, stamens, velvet leaves, millinery feathers and other embellishments.

Anne Barge

404-872-8070
www.AnneBarge.com

Anne Barge bridal gowns are classic designs with museum-quality beading and embroidery. Anne's designs are inspired by vintage couture and feature timeless references translated to modern silhouettes.

The Estate

3109 Piedmont Road
Atlanta, GA 30305
404-869-8858
www.alegendaryevent.com

A Legendary Event owns and manages The Estate event venue comprised of a fully restored antebellum mansion, ballroom and gardens. A Legendary Event is a full-service event catering and design company with over fifteen years of experience.

Ivy & Aster

646-470-4489
www.ivyandaster.com

One part sweet and one part sass, Ivy & Aster offers bridal, reception and social dresses for today's modern bride.

JEREMY HARWELL

Harwell Photography

Atlanta, Georgia
404-245-1028
www.harwellphotography.com

This boutique wedding and editorial studio specializes in fine art images.

Kelly's Closet

1649 McLendon Avenue NE
Atlanta, GA 30307
404-377-9923
www.kellyscloset.net

Kravet Fabrics

225 Central Avenue
South Bethpage, NY 11714
800-648-5728
www.kravet.com

Fabrics, furniture and trimmings available through design trade only.

Nikole Morrow-Pettus

Master Makeup Artist
Van Michael Salon
39 W. Paces Ferry Road
Atlanta, GA 30305
404-237-4664

Complete makeup needs for weddings and editorial and media events.

Swarovski

www.swarovski.com

We use Swarovski crystals on almost everything we create. Swarovski produces some of the finest quality crystals in the world.

ACKNOWLEDGMENTS

This book was produced with the help of a talented team of creative people who helped us to realize our vision.

Our amazing photographer, Jeremy Harwell: Thank you for your golden eye.

Donna Jassman: For transforming our sketches into finished artwork using your superb design skills.

James Jasper Fason: For your knowledge, time and contract advice.

Dresses: Anne Barge, Ivy & Aster, Kelly's Closet

Hair: Kathy Tepedino

Makeup: Nikole Morrow-Pettus

Models: Elizabeth Rowland and Laura Weinzettel

Location: The Estate on Piedmont. A big thank you to Tony Conway and Amy Bending for your gracious hospitality and support.

A special thanks to editor Noel Rivera and publisher F + W Media.

To our families and friends who always give us the love, laughter and unwavering support that allows us to create beautiful things: Our most heartfelt thanks.

To the ladies "D": Donna, Darlene and Jamie. And our friends to "dyed" for: Brooke, Calista and Shelia. Many thanks for support over the many creative years.

To all the editors and clients who have been so amazingly wonderful to us. Thank you!

Nicholas Kniel

For more than a decade, Las Vegas-born designer Nicholas Kniel has been a purveyor of fine ribbons and embellishments. Nicholas started his career creating visual displays for large corporations and couture boutiques. With a bachelor's degree in fashion design from the American College, Nicholas then turned his talents to couture evening and wedding gown design.

In 2000, Nicholas opened his boutique, Nicholas Kniel Fine Ribbons & Embellishments, in Atlanta, Georgia. The boutique and online shop serve as great design resources for many people around the world.

Nicholas Kniel's ribbon flowers have been featured in *Martha Stewart Weddings*, *Traditional Home*, *Victoria* and *Sew Beautiful* magazines. Over the years, Nicholas has custom-made countless ribbon adornments for clients, including those used on costumes by the Guthrie Theatre in Minneapolis, for brides and the bridal industry, for milliners all over the world and, notably, the rock goddess Courtney Love.

Timothy Wright

"My interests are akin to a cabinet of curiosities," says Timothy Wright, artist, designer, writer, and native southerner living in Atlanta. He attended the Atlanta College of Art and studied fine painting, developing a taste for the esoteric and obscure in the process. His paintings, prints and drawings have been exhibited publicly and are held in private collections across the country. He has donated his time and artistry to the Atlanta Ballet, joining other artists in creating works of art from ballet slippers for the ballet's toe-shoe fund. His poetry has been published in various print and online magazines and literary journals, and he occasionally participates in group poetry readings. Much of his work is inspired by the natural world, and he collects natural objects, vintage paper ephemera and antique photographs. Timothy loves textiles and teaches ribbon work classes at Nicholas Kniel. He is the co-author of *Ribbon: The Art of Adornment*.

Jeremy Harwell

Jeremy has been in love with photography for a very long time. He started as a photojournalist working for newspapers, then moved on to portrait photography before landing at Ralph Lauren, where he spent eight years working as the creative director for the New York stores.

The many stops along the way taught him a great deal, and his style is a mix of all he has experienced. Like Tennyson said in *Ulysses*, Jeremy says, "I am a part of all I have met."

Currently, he lives in Georgia and has run his own wedding studio for the last eight years. He has been published in *Martha Stewart Weddings*, *Modern Bride*, *Inside Weddings*, *Destination Weddings*, *Southern Weddings*, *PDN*, *Atlanta Weddings*, *Weddings Unveiled* and *Bride's Magazine*.

www.fwmedia.com

17   16   15   14   13   5   4   3   2   1

Distributed in Canada by Fraser Direct
100 Armstrong Avenue
Georgetown, ON, Canada L7G 5S4
Tel: (905) 877-4411

Distributed in the U.K. and Europe by F&W MEDIA INTERNATIONAL
Brunel House, Newton Abbot, Devon, TQ12 4PU, England
Tel: (+44) 1626 323200, Fax: (+44) 1626 323319
Email: enquiries@fwmedia.com

Distributed in Australia by Capricorn Link
P.O. Box 704, S. Windsor NSW, 2756 Australia
Tel: (02) 4560-1600   Fax: (02) 4577-5288
Email: books@capricornlink.com.au

ISBN 10: 1-4463-0461-2
ISBN 13: 978-1-4463-0461-7

SRN: T1307

metric conversion chart

TO CONVERT	TO	MULTIPLY BY
Inches	Centimeters	2.54
Centimeters	Inches	0.4
Feet	Centimeters	30.5
Centimeters	Feet	0.03
Yards	Meters	0.9
Meters	Yards	1.1

Edited by Noel Rivera

Designed by Kelly Pace

Photography by Jeremy Harwell

Art Direction + Styling by Nicholas Kniel

Illustrations by Timothy Wright

Digitized Illustrations by Donna Jassman

Production Coordinated by Greg Nock

INDEX

TRY THE BEAUTIFUL DESIGNS IN SOME OF OUR OTHER FABRIC AND RIBBON EMBELLISHMENT TITLES!

ADORNMENTS
Sew & Create Accessories with Fabric, Lace & Beads
Myra Callan

Myra Callan of Twigs and Honey shows readers how to create pretty accessories with feathers, lace, silk flowers, crystals, beads and more in twenty tutorials for pretty, accessible projects with a lush, romantic look and feel that will spark readers' imaginations.

ISBN-13: 978-1-4402-2934-3
SRN: W7141

RIBBONWORK: THE COMPLETE GUIDE
Techniques for Making Ribbon Flowers and Trimmings
Helen Gibb

Learn to make vintage ribbon flowers and leaves, and be inspired to create incredibly beautiful projects. Using the detailed step-by-step instructions, diagrams and photos, you'll soon be on your way to making ribbon flower compositions for your hats, albums, pillows, dolls, quilts and more.

ISBN-13: 978-0-8734-9750-3
SRN: RWPR

MORE SEWING WITH WHIMSY
Kari Mecca

Kari Mecca demonstrates how to create even more fabulous embellishments and trims in *More Sewing with Whimsy*. The book provides three full-size patterns for girl's sizes 2–6, with variations for six more looks and even more project and embellishment ideas to add personality to handmade and ready-made items.

ISBN-13: 978-1-8780-4861-5
SRN: V0791

CHECK OUT MORE OF OUR EXCITING TITLES AT SEWDAILY.COM!